BF 1321 .T38

Learning to Use Extrasensory Perception

Learning to Use Extrasensory Perception

Charles T. Tart

29708

The
University
of Chicago
Press

Chicago and
London

The University of Chicago Press, Chicago 60637
The University of Chicago Press, Ltd., London
© 1975, 1976 by The University of Chicago
All rights reserved. Published 1976
Printed in the United States of America
80 79 78 77 76   987654321

Library of Congress Cataloging in Publication Data

Tart, Charles T   1937–
    Learning to use extrasensory perception.

    Bibliography: p.
    Includes index.
    1.   Extrasensory perception—Study and teaching.
I.   Title.
BF1321.T38   133.8   75–43233
ISBN 0–226–78991–8

CHARLES T. TART is Professor of Psychology at the
University of California, Davis. Professor Tart's
publications include *Altered States of Consciousness;
On Being Stoned: A Psychological Study of Marijuana
Intoxication; Transpersonal Psychologies; States of
Consciousness;* and *Studies of Psi,* as well as many
scientific articles.

Contents

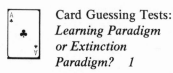

v

Preface

One of parapsychology's greatest problems, pointed out by critics and defenders alike, is the lack of a repeatable experiment. This is not quite true: we have *statistical* repeatability. For example, roughly one out of every three experiments conducted by members of the Parapsychological Association obtained significant evidence for ESP (Tart, 1973a), and certain effects, such as the sheep-goat effect or decline effects, have been obtained in many experiments. Yet we cannot say with any certainty that if you carry out such and such a procedure you will almost certainly obtain significant amounts of ESP.

Critics have cited this lack of a repeatable experiment as arguing against the existence of psi phenomena, a fallacious argument that will not concern us here. More important, the lack of a reliable way of getting psi performance is a serious drawback to understanding ESP. Most experimentation in science consists of starting with a poorly understood but occurring phenomenon and then varying the conditions under which it occurs in order to understand its nature. This leads to better formulations (theories) of phenomena, more sophisticated experimental work, etc. This is scientific progress. But if you can't be sure of getting any ESP, or if it occurs only sporadically, your ability to study it by varying conditions is greatly weakened, and progress is slow and erratic, with much waste of effort.

An analogy I have often used in speaking about this problem is that parapsychology today is where the science of electricity was for most of mankind's history. You had two electrical phenomena, lightning and weak static effects. Lightning flashes were spectacular and had great effects; unfortunately, any particular lightning flash occurred unpredictably and was over in an instant, making study difficult. You also had the fact that a piece of amber, rubbed with fur, would sometimes pick up a feather. It was a very weak and erratic force, it couldn't do much, and it often wouldn't manifest for non-apparent reasons (which, in retrospect, we can understand as things like relative humidity, etc.). We understood almost nothing about electricity with these two effects for most of our history.

Then the battery was invented. It couldn't compete with lightning for power and effect, but it was totally predictable and reliable, giving a steady strong flow of the phenomenon of electricity that amber and fur never gave. Now one could set up apparatus and invest energy in study and be amply repaid. Progress has been enormous.

In parapsychology we have our lightning: spontaneous phenomena, temperamental psychics, spectacular experiments that don't repeat. We have our amber: one out of three experiments showing statistically significant, but *practically negligible*, ESP effects. We need our parapsychological battery.

Our great need is to learn how to train subjects so we can have a reliable flow of ESP. This is not for the purpose of convincing skeptics, for conviction is seldom a rational matter, but so that our studies of how psi manifests, and what affects it, will yield profitable returns and enable us to understand it. The theory and studies reported in this book are an attempt to develop the parapsychological battery.

Chapter 1, first published as a journal article in 1966, is my original attempt to apply learning theory to ESP performance. In the years since then, a number of studies have strongly supported the application, and these are reviewed in chapter 2. The third chapter presents a small-scale study of the application which highlights some of the complexities, such as psi-missing, that an expanded theory will have to deal with. The heart of this book is the fourth chapter, where Dana Redington and I describe a major study which demonstrates that the feedback called for in the learning theory application can largely eliminate the usual decline in ESP performance and produce learning in some subjects. Notes on the behavior and internal processes of the five best subjects of the most successful experimenter, Gaines Thomas, are presented in chapter 5. Implications are discussed in chapter 6, and a more theoretical look at the internal processes involved in learning to use ESP is presented in chapter 7. Chapter 8 is a brief summary chapter.

The Ten-Choice Trainer used in the main study is described in Appendix 1 for the benefit of researchers who wish to build similar devices. As an illustration of more sophisticated electronics technology for such training instruments, appendix 2 (reprinted from a journal article) gives a description of ESPATESTER, a device I developed simultaneously with the original application of learning theory to ESP to facilitate this sort of research.

Writing reports on parapsychological experiments has a special hazard, viz., so much detail is required that the reader may get bogged down in it and lose track of the main points. Unfortunately, this is necessary. For the serious reader who wants to check my interpretation of data, or consider his own alternative interpretations, precise detail is necessary. Too, many biased critics of parapsychological data invent all sorts of hypotheses to explain away results and tie these to any lack of information, so parapsychologists have developed a certain defensive level of precise detail to try to avoid giving false openings for criticism. The present book, covering the basic application of learning theory to ESP and reporting one pilot study and a three-phase major study, is filled with necessary detail. While I have tried to keep the writing clear, the reader may get sidetracked on detail at times. The brief summary at the end (chapter 8) can be consulted if you lose track of where we are going!

A briefer version of this book first appeared as a Parapsychology Foundation Monograph, under the title "The Application of Learning Theory to Extrasensory Perception" (New York, 1975). The present text revises and considerably expands that earlier monograph and corrects a few minor errors in it, such as the inappropriate use of one-tailed statistical tests in analysis of results on the early pilot study and the later Training Study.

I am convinced that the application of learning theory, illustrated in this book, is a powerful tool for reliably producing and studying ESP. I hope that other workers will develop the theory and application even further than this initial attempt.

A preliminary version of these results was circulated to colleagues, and I would like to especially acknowledge helpful comments by Charles Honorton, J. B. Rhine, Gertrude Schmeidler, and Helmut Schmidt.

Learning to Use Extrasensory Perception

1   Card Guessing Tests:
Learning Paradigm or Extinction Paradigm?

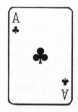

In an excellent article, Rhea White (1964) has pointed out some striking differences between the conditions in modern card guessing tests of ESP and in older, but often more significant, experiments in which the subjects had time to use and analyze their internal imagery and other psychological processes. Her plea that we should evaluate and study the conditions of these older experiments in order to understand the means whereby ESP impressions can come into consciousness is one that should be heeded by all workers in this area.

White's article reflects a steadily growing disillusionment among workers in the field about the value of the standard card guessing tests of ESP.[1] This disillusionment is realistic in many ways, for we seem to have about exhausted this technique. Despite many interesting and minor studies which remain to be done, one can be legitimately skeptical about the use of a technique where marginally significant results are the norm, where we are dealing with very weak manifestations of the underlying phenomena, and where the magnitude of this manifestation has not increased over decades of experimentation.

Important as the need for totally new approaches to studying ESP is, however, at the same time we should be doing *more* card tests because *the card guessing tests have, by and large, never been used in a way which would bring out their possible potential.* This chapter

Reprinted from the *Journal of the American Society for Psychical Research*, 60 (1966): 46-55, by permission of the American Society for Psychical Research.

will point out a basic flaw in our card guessing test procedures and discuss ways of rectifying it.

The assumption behind almost all ESP testing has been that we are trying to *detect* an extant capacity. It may be more profitable, however, to assume that whatever this capacity is, it is latent in the subject and he must *learn* to use it within the context of the experimental situation. Let us now consider some basic facts about learning.

Learning

Learning refers to a hypothetical change within an organism (whether animal or human) which is reflected or manifested as a change (improvement) in performance during the course of practice at some task. Almost all learning takes place in situations where the correct response is rewarded on *each* trial and incorrect responses are not rewarded, or may even be punished. Thus someone attempting to learn to play a scale on the piano is rewarded by a smile from his teacher (and, perhaps, the satisfaction of the harmony) if he runs through it correctly, but is met with disapproval (and disharmony) if he is incorrect. Reward, especially with human subjects, can also be conceived of as feedback of information on the correctness or incorrectness of performance and, insofar as the subject is motivated to perform correctly, knowledge that his response was correct is rewarding.

Two typical laboratory learning situations will illustrate some important facts about the learning process. As a case of animal learning, we have a pigeon inside a soundproof box. In one corner is a trough where pellets of food may appear as they are released by an automatic mechanism. As the pigeon is hungry, food is rewarding. On one wall of the box is a key that the pigeon may press with his beak, and over the key is a red light. We want the pigeon to press the key whenever the red light is on, but not when it is off, so a circuit is set up such that key presses when the light is on drop food pellets into the trough, while presses when the light is off have no effect.

When first put in the box, the pigeon will be agitated. After calming down, the pigeon will sooner or later press the key while the light is on, by "accident."He will be rewarded *immediately* by a food pellet. Over the course of a few hours, we will find that the pigeon pecks rapidly at the key whenever the light is on, and not when it is off. He has been rewarded for the correct response. Because his behavior is now correct, we infer that he has learned the proper response to the red light, viz., key pressing.

Take a human subject and have him extend his hand behind a curtain to hold a metal stylus. Put the tip of the stylus in a simple maze constructed so that whenever the stylus goes off the correct path of the maze it will sound an electric buzzer. Otherwise the subject has no way of knowing when he is on or off the correct pathway. Now instruct the subject to try to trace his way through the maze (which he cannot see) without going off the path. On his early trials he will make many deviations from the path, but whenever he hears the buzzer he will draw back the stylus from that direction. Eventually (assuming the maze is not too complex) he will be able to trace through the maze without any mistakes. The reward here is the lack of a buzzer sounding, for the buzzer is the feedback signal that he has made a mistake. Behaviorally we may analyze the responses of the human subject and the pigeon in the same way, viz., how many trials are needed to reach a criterion of perfect performance. Introspectively, the human subject can provide other data: he might report that the task was difficult, that he had to coordinate his hand movements with some sort of image he was developing in his mind, and that while he might not be able to describe just what he did to get through the maze without activating the buzzer, he nevertheless learned to do it. This last point is particularly important, for there are many things we learn to do in life which we cannot verbalize to others, or even adequately conceive of ourselves—try describing just how you ride a bicycle, for instance. The operation of ESP is probably no exception to this, i.e., it is possible for a person to use it without being able to understand or explain just how it operates.

Now a number of factors affect the course of learning over and above the simple presence or absence of reward or feedback, such as the subject's motivation to learn and his state of health. A very important factor is the time relationship between the subject's response and the reward or feedback. Almost all studies of learning show that learning is slower and less effective as the interval between response and reward increases. With lower organisms, particularly, a fairly lengthy interval between response and reward results in no learning at all, i.e., the organism never emits the correct response with greater than chance frequency. In general, intervals between response and reward or feedback are optimal if they are of less than a second, and learning falls off rapidly in many instances if these intervals reach even a few seconds.

The opposite of learning is extinction, i.e., the correct response in a situation appearing less and less frequently, and finally failing to appear altogether. The typical laboratory procedure for producing extinction of a learned response is simply to stop rewarding each such response as it is emitted by the organism. Or one can give the reward, but give it in such a way that it is ineffective for the particular organism, e.g., by making the response-reward interval so long that the organism no longer "associates" the reward with the correct response.

Repeated Guessing Tests

In this light, let us examine the typical card guessing situation as used in almost all parapsychological experimentation up through the 1950's. The subject comes in, with some motivation to do well on the test (whether "doing well" means scoring positively for sheep or negatively for goats). He is then required to give a large number of responses (guesses), usually twenty-five, and some of these responses are correct, while others are incorrect. The correct responses may occur with greater than chance frequency; in fact, they frequently do on the initial run. After the subject has emitted a large number of responses, the experimenter usually tells him which were correct and which incorrect. *There has been no reward or feedback immediately after each response.* Indeed, the feedback coming after such a large number of trials is probably completely ineffective.[2] What little reward there is (feeling gratified at scoring above chance) tends to be associated with the entire run rather than with the individual responses. This paradigm, then, is basically an *extinction* paradigm, and is well suited to eliminate correct responses occurring with a greater than chance frequency.

Recall the learning situation with the pigeon, where a food pellet was produced *immediately* after each correct response. If we superimposed the card guessing paradigm, the same pigeon would be put in the box and after it had emitted a large number of responses, correct and incorrect, the experimenter would give it a handful of food! No psychologist would expect the pigeon to learn the correct response; in fact, the key pecking response would remain at an extremely low frequency because it would not become associated with the reward.

If we superimposed the card guessing paradigm on the maze learning situation with the human, we would disconnect the buzzer but tell the subject to trace the maze and not make any mistakes. After he had tried this a number of times we would inform him that he had made mistakes, and to try again! As with the pigeon, no learning would be likely to result.

Looking at the typical card guessing experiment introspectively, on each guessing trial the subject is responding to a host of internal cues, many of them probably not clearly represented in consciousness and many of them probably extremely transient. In going over his results with him at the end of twenty-five trials, we are asking him to do a rather heroic task, viz., to recall the particular set of amorphous feelings and sensations associated with each one of the twenty-five trials and to retrospectively associate these amorphous, transient feelings with this late knowledge of results. Moreover, as White (1964) has pointed out, the interval between trials has typically been much too short for the subject to attempt to clarify his internal feelings and perceptions in the first place.

Any psychologist, if asked to have *any* organism learn under conditions of massed, unrewarded trials, followed by occasional rewards which cannot be associated with particular responses by the organism, will throw up his hands in disgust and wonder where the idea for such a bizarre joke came from.

Not only does the typical card guessing paradigm fit this theoretical model of the extinction paradigm, but the empirical results bear it out (Pratt, 1949). Almost all subjects, no matter how much above chance expectancy they are at first, eventually, with repeated testing, come down to chance expectancy (another of the factors which is leading to discouragement with card guessing tests). We have, unknowingly yet systematically, been extinguishing the operation of ESP in our subjects. Indeed, one might cite as an argument for the existence and lawfulness of ESP the fact that we are able to extinguish it by conventional procedures!

What can be done about it?

Training ESP

What is needed is an experimental procedure in which (a) the subject's guesses have virtually immediate consequences, i.e., knowledge of results and/or reward (or punishment) on every trial; (b) the testing situation is intrinsically motivating enough to the subject so that some ESP is operative in the first place; and (c) the mechanics of target selection, recording, and presentation of feedback, reward, or punishment are unobtrusive so as not to distract the subject or the agent. Note that requirement (b) brings out an assumption basic to the argument of this chapter, viz., that the subject will utilize ESP in conjunction with some of his responses; otherwise there is nothing to reinforce! If a subject is simply guessing, immediate reinforcement of correct responses amounts to reinforcing randomly varying factors of no value and there will be no learning to use ESP. If, on the other hand, the subject is using ESP in conjunction with some of his responses, this is a constant factor that will be reinforced and we would expect learning to occur.

The situation is somewhat complicated by the fact that even a subject who *is* utilizing ESP in conjunction with some of his guesses is also being reinforced for some responses that are pure guesses but are correct by chance alone. One might think of this as "noise," and this consideration leads us to predict three general outcomes for experiments using immediate reinforcement: (a) for a subject who shows no ESP at first (indicated by chance-level scoring), there is nothing to be reinforced, so he will continue to score at a chance level no matter how long the experiment is continued; (b) for a subject who shows only a little ESP at first, the infrequent reinforcement of ESP responses and the more frequent reinforcement of chance responses may not allow learning to begin before extinction has started, i.e., there is far more reinforcement of "noise" than of "signal," so he will soon start to score at a chance level; (c) for a subject who shows a large number of ESP responses at first, their systematic reinforcement should outweigh the reward of chance responses, and learning should take place as manifested by an overall increase in scoring level with further trials. What the exact dividing line is between (b) and (c) constitutes an empirical problem that future research must solve.

There have been some experimental setups in the past which have come close to getting away from this extinction paradigm. The procedure of allowing subjects to check the calls they felt sure were correct, as in the research of Humphrey and Nicol (1955), was one approach, but here in many cases the feedback of correctness or incorrectness did not come until the end of the run; thus it would have been difficult for the subject to remember just what feelings caused him to check a particular call, so that he could learn to recognize them clearly in the future. Some experiments have been done, using open decks, where the experimenter tells the subject whether he is right or wrong after each call. These experiments would seem to fit a learning rather than an extinction paradigm, yet in retrospect it is questionable whether the feedback of correctness or incorrectness was very rapid—in dealing with such a nebulous and poorly understood phenomenon it may be that the difference between half-a-second and one-second intervals between response and feedback is crucial. Moreover, the mechanics of the experimental procedure in these studies (randomizing, recording responses in duplicate, etc.) may have been a factor detracting from the opportunity for learning.

After reading an earlier draft of this chapter, Laura Dale was kind enough to call my attention to a series of experiments carried out at the A.S.P.R. in which the subject did receive quick knowledge of results. The first of these (Murphy & Taves, 1942) was one in which the agent pressed a switch to give a signal to the subject as to whether he had been right or wrong on each trial. Considering the mechanics of this procedure, however, the feedback was delayed and variable, and thus not well suited for an initial investigation into the effect of knowledge of results on learning to use ESP. In three later experiments the apparatus was modified so that a bell rang immediately if the subject pushed the switch corresponding to a correct guess, thus giving immediate reinforcement of correctness. In the first of these three experiments (Taves & Dale, 1943), the authors reported a marked decline effect rather than any learning. This result does not, however, constitute a demonstration that immediate knowledge of results, or reinforcement, fails to help a subject to use ESP. As pointed out above, there is probably some critical ratio of correct responses due to ESP versus correct responses due to chance which must be reached or exceeded early in the guessing so that learning can begin before the ESP responses begin to extinguish. Apparently this ratio was not reached in the Taves and Dale study. Nor was it reached in the two later experiments (Dale et al., 1944; Taves et al., 1943), as the authors reported there were no significant results either in overall scoring or in terms of decline effects; thus there was probably no ESP to be reinforced.

A number of mechanical devices have been proposed in the past which produced random targets and automatically scored responses (Smith et al., 1963; Stewart, 1959; Taves, 1939; Webster, 1949). Unfortunately, most of these devices never saw any use to speak of and many of them were actually rather awkward to operate, so that a quick reward of responses would have been difficult to accomplish.[3] A modern device which would easily allow the use of quick reinforcement (Cutten, 1961) has been proposed, but no one has backed its construction. Another modern device (Tart, 1966b and appendix 2), designed to allow all the techniques of reinforcement used in present-day psychology to be applied, has failed to receive backing for construction.[4] Apparently the reaction against card guessing tests has dampened enthusiasm for such testing aids. However, they are absolutely necessary if we are to turn card guessing tests into a learning situation (using animal or human subjects) instead of an extinction procedure, because manual procedures are probably too slow, cumbersome, and distracting to both experimenter and subject.

A properly designed testing aid, which automatically generated random targets and scored the subject's responses, could easily be set up to do all of the following: (a) allow the subject to respond as slowly as he wishes, thus giving him a chance to clarify his internal feelings and imagery, or to work rapidly, almost automatically; (b) reward the subject for correct responses, with fixed or variable intervals between response and reward, on a constant or variable reward schedule; (c) provide reward as straight information feedback (a buzzer for correct responses, say), or provide something like coins falling from a dispenser on each correct response; (d) punish the subject for incorrect responses, either in an informational feedback way or by something like electric shock or monetary fines. Other techniques could be programmed in, but basically the point is that by the use of modern apparatus all the highly developed techniques of learning psychology and operant conditioning could be applied to guessing situations, and quite possibly we would find that subjects could learn to perform at more and more significant levels over time instead of dropping off to chance.

As an example of what this sort of feedback might accomplish, consider the old and remarkably successful experiment of Brugmans and his colleagues (1922, pp. 396–408), where the agents were able to continually observe the movements of the subject's hand as he attempted to locate the square to which the agents were trying to direct him. Whenever the subject moved his hand in the right direction the agents could intensify their "sending," but whenever it went in the wrong direction they could try another technique and thus continuously vary their "sending" behaviors in accordance with what seemed to produce the best responses in the subject. This sort of experiment could easily be carried out today, and now that closed-circuit TV systems are reasonably priced, the agents could be miles away, totally eliminating problems of sensory cues. They could jump about and shout if they thought it helped, and work up a tremendous emotional involvement in their task!

Giving both the subject and the agent a chance to learn to use their psi capacities should be more fruitful than either approach alone.

Considering the literature reviewed above, then, subjects have simply never been given an adequate chance to learn to use their ESP abilities, especially those high-scoring subjects where the use of immediate reinforcement techniques would be most profitable. Undoubtedly there are some other experiments in the scattered literature of parapsychology which come closer to a learning paradigm than I (a relative newcomer to the field) know of; what is most amazing to me as a psychologist, however, is this well-nigh universal use of an extinction paradigm. The main point of this chapter is a plea to workers in the field to give the learning paradigm a fair try before abandoning guessing tests entirely.

It should be noted that these comments are not a *sophisticated* analysis of the card guessing method as a learning situation; rather, they are based on knowledge that can be picked up in elementary textbooks on psychology (Hilgard, 1962; Morgan, 1956). Because we have been absorbed in the idea of detection instead of learning, we have actually been working against ourselves in terms of producing the phenomena we want to study. It is to be hoped that the application of these basic principles of learning will be carried out, for the crucial problem in parapsychology today is to produce the phenomena we want to study at a much higher level than the marginal one we are used to, and the proper application of the psychology of learning may be one way of accomplishing this.

2   Studies of the Learning Theory Application by Others, 1964–75

I discussed the possibility of teaching steady ESP performance by the application of immediate feedback with many people, including other parapsychologists, and, with the exception of Russell Targ and Herbert Puryear, who had had similar thoughts, the idea apparently fell on deaf ears. In 1966 I put it in the form of an article, now reprinted as chapter 1 of this book. The article outlined the basic learning theory application to ESP, and further stressed an important point, viz., that a subject would have to have some demonstrable ESP ability to begin with, or the application of immediate feedback would not be useful. That is, if there is no talent to reinforce, the application of feedback and reinforcement will be of limited value. If the subject has a good deal of ESP ability to begin with, learning would be predicted to be fairly rapid. At intermediate levels of ESP ability, we would expect either increased variability, as a subject tried different, partially effective strategies, or stabilization of performance for some time, but probably not learning. The fact that a subject is being reinforced by chance very often in a repeated guessing experiment constitutes a kind of noise, and, coupled with the boredom of long testing, this noise may be sufficient to sap the subject's motivation and/or confuse him, so that learning does not occur. I could find no material in the psychological literature comparable to the standard ESP card guessing tests that would enable me to theoretically predict what the level of initial ESP had to be before learning could occur under feedback conditions, so finding this "talent threshold" is an empirical problem.[1] I shall propose an approximate empirical solution in chapter 6.

One rough way of expressing the need for some ESP ability to begin with, if reinforcement is to be effective in producing learning, is to predict that there should be a positive correlation between measures of subjects' ESP ability and the slope of the regression lines fitted to their performance under conditions of immediate reinforcement. This is only rough because a correlation coefficient assumes linearity, and there may be something like a step-function here, i.e., below the necessary talent threshold, amount of ESP will correlate with slope only moderately.

Note carefully that the learning theory application is about *individual* subjects, and data must be analyzed on a subject by subject basis, not for the group of subjects as a whole. This is necessary because of the talent threshold concept. If you happened to have a group of subjects most of whom were below the talent threshold, their results could swamp those of one or two who were above the talent threshold and showed learning. Because of persistent misunderstanding of this point by colleagues, I emphasize that the learning theory application predicts that *individual subjects who are above the talent threshold* can show learning under conditions of immediate feedback. The only prediction being made about groups is that of a positive correlation between overall ESP ability and the slopes of the performance curves.

Also in 1966 I published a design for an automated ESP testing and training machine (ESPATESTER) that not only made convenient testing in repeated guessing situations easy, but provided immediate feedback so that learning could occur (Tart, 1966b and appendix 2). I built an ESPATESTER while at the University of Virginia Medical School and informally had several dozen subjects try their hands at it, but since none of them showed significant ESP scores to begin with, these results did not constitute any kind of test of the application of learning theory to ESP.

The publication of the theory in 1966 created some interest among parapsychologists, and a number of experimenters incorporated immediate feedback of results into experimental designs, although it was not always assessed as an independent variable. The general finding seemed to be that no spectacular results followed from providing immediate feedback, so interest in the theory waned. As will be shown, however, almost all of the published studies were inadequate tests of the learning theory application, for they dealt with subjects who showed only small amounts of ESP, or none at all; thus they failed to give proper recognition to the provision of the theory that calls for some minimal talent threshold before feedback produces clear learning. We shall see that this waning of interest was premature and invalid.

However, some two dozen scattered studies have appeared which give substantial support to the learning theory application and which shall be reviewed here. I have restricted myself to studies with human subjects.

Because of the theoretical importance of the requirement that a subject have some initial ESP ability before immediate feedback can be expected to do much (owing to the inherent extinction effects from chance reinforcement), the published literature will be reviewed under three broad headings. First, we shall look at studies in which there was no apparent ESP, i.e., where the overall group results did not differ significantly from chance expectation. Second, we shall examine studies using moderately talented subjects, i.e., where the overall group results were significant at the .01 level and the like, but where we would not generally expect significant results from an examination of the scores of individual subjects. Third, we shall consider studies in which individuals scored significantly. These are rough groupings, of course, and partially contaminated by possible learning effects. Ideally there should have been measures of individuals' ESP talent levels before they were put in an immediate feedback situation,[2] but this was seldom the case.

It will be difficult to compare absolute scoring levels across studies as ESP tests with different P values were used, ranging from binary targets ($P = .5$) to exact hits on playing cards ($P = 1/52$). A similar percentage of hits for targets with different P values does not mean the same thing. Scoring 2 percent above chance expectation on a ten-choice task, e.g., implies a more difficult discrimination than the same 2 percent above chance on a two-choice task. I shall try to give an idea of the magnitude of the ESP operating in various studies where appropriate, but this can only be approximate, for a completely satisfactory measure does not yet exist.

The studies reviewed below had many other variables functioning in addition to the presence of feedback; indeed many of them were not explicitly designed to assess the effects of feedback. Nevertheless I shall focus on this factor to show the existence of widespread support for the learning theory application.

All of the studies reviewed had adequate safeguards against factors other than ESP, such as sensory leakage or recording errors, accounting for non-chance scoring, except for some specific cases which I shall discuss.

Studies with Subjects Who Have No Apparent ESP

Seven studies have appeared whose overall results do not show significant hitting above chance but which employed immediate feedback. The learning theory application does not definitely predict learning in such cases, since subjects are below the necessary talent threshold for the learning process to predominate over the extinction process. The situation is a little ambiguous, of course, for some subjects may appear to be untalented in initial testing but have latent abilities that, if motivation is high, might be tapped after a period of training with feedback.

The first such study was carried out by Beloff (1969). He used the Edinburgh Electronic ESP Tester (Beloff and Regan, 1969), a five-choice device providing immediate feedback. Twenty men and 20 women, university students, did five runs of 25 trials each, with immediate feedback via the correct target lamp lighting. The subjects showed no ESP and there was no improvement with practice. This kind of result is consistent with the learning theory application, but in a trivial way.

Banham (1970) had 22 college student subjects work with a toy slot machine. They had to drop a marble into one of four slots. One outlet, selected at random, was blocked on each trial so the marble would not roll out, and the subjects were to try to drop the marble into this slot. Whether or not the marble rolled out almost immediately was the feedback. Both men and women scored higher in the second half of the experiment than in the first, the women significantly so ($P < .001$), but the scores of the group as a whole did not differ significantly from chance. Although no details are provided, Banham also mentions that a post hoc analysis of another experiment (presumably like this one) showed a similar result.

In a replication of her earlier study, again reported only in a short abstract, Banham (1973) reported no significant differences between scores in two sequential 100-trial blocks for 30 college student subjects. There was a typical decline effect when the first and last ten trials within each 100-trial block were examined. Banham attributes this to the feedback, although why she does this is not clear, since such declines are the typical result in non-feedback, repeated guessing studies.

Beloff and Bate (1971), impressed by others' significant ESP scores on the Schmidt machine (reviewed later), which incidentally provides immediate feedback even though Schmidt has not conceptualized such feedback as important, ran four subjects for fairly extended series (2,900 trials or more) on their five-choice Edinburgh Electronic ESP Tester.[3] The subjects had various numbers of trials trying to guess the state of the machine (clairvoyance) in real time or to predict its forthcoming state (precognition). For some runs feedback was immediate, for others the feedback lamps were disconnected. These four conditions were intermixed throughout the series.

Beloff and Bate found no statistically significant ESP for any of these four subjects, and had non-significant indications that their subjects did better when immediate feedback was withheld. They do not provide performance curves under the various conditions, however, making it difficult to evaluate the feedback and non-feedback conditions adequately. They do provide overall (conditions intermingled) cumulative response curves for their subjects, and, using this graphical data, I approximately extracted actual score deviations above and below chance expectation for the blocks of 20 runs (500 trials) they presented their data in. I calculated the slopes of the performance curves for deviations for their subjects. One subject (R.S.) showed a significant decline effect (slope = -.461, i.e., he was declining about one ESP response every 40 runs or 1,000 trials), but the three others were showing positive slopes (.517, .481, and .600 for M.W., E.B., and M.M., respectively), one of which was suggestively significant (for E.B., $P < .10$), even though their overall scores were low. The reason the slopes were positive was that each of these three subjects showed scores below chance at the beginning of their training. Cases of positive learning slopes coming about through initial psi-missing, followed by chance scores or hitting, are complex and not covered by simple learning theory (see the discussion in chapter 3).

Thouless (1971) attempted to train himself on the four-choice Schmidt machine (Schmidt, 1970). Although he felt there was a suggestively positive trend through his twelfth session, it was followed by a decline on the thirteenth session, just before he had to terminate the experiment as the machine became unavailable, and his overall scores were not significantly above chance.

Perhaps the most literal application of immediate feedback was in a study by Drucker and Drewes (1976). Fifty young children performed an ESP task of guessing what color m&m's candy was in the experimenter's closed hand. The experimenter opened her hand immediately after the guess, providing almost immediate feedback of information, and the child was then allowed, if correct, to pick an identical color m&m's from another bag and eat it right away or save it for later. Five different colors of candy were used, drawn from a closed bag of 20 of each color; after each response the m&m's were replaced, to avoiding changing P values. Each child completed two runs of 25 guesses each.

The primary focus of this study was on the relation of cognitive development stage to ESP scoring. The experimenters divided the children into high- and low-IQ groups (splitting above and below the mean), and found that the high-IQ children showed a small but significant improvement from the first to the second run ($P < .01$), while the low-IQ children showed a suggestive but non-significant decrement from the first to the second run.

Jampolsky and Haight (1975) had children, aged 9–13, carry out 192 runs of 25 trials each on the Aquarius Model 100 ESP Trainer (described fully in chapter 4). They were divided into two groups of 10 each, one group composed of hyperkinetic children, the other composed of normal ones. Although better ESP scores were expected from the hyperkinetics, neither group scored significantly above chance and there were no significant differences between the groups. One child (a hyperkinetic) showed a positive slope indicative of learning that was significant at the .05 level, but, given that 20 slope tests were carried out, this may well have occurred by chance.

I should note that I believe young children (preferably of preschool age) may make the best possible subjects for ESP research, *if* you can keep them interested in the experimental task, for I suspect we are all born with a biological endowment for ESP that is largely suppressed in the course of enculturation. Jampolsky's and Haight's children were old enough to be well "socialized," but we still need preselection for ESP talent, even with children, to adequately test the learning theory application.

The general picture, then, is that of immediate feedback often having no effect on the performance of subjects who apparently have no ESP talent; yet, in spite of the fact that we do not expect it, some subjects seem to show some learning. This finding is retrospectively compatible with the learning theory application, for it is likely that an occasional mildly talented subject would show up in otherwise unselected, untalented groups.

Studies with Mildly Talented Subjects

The criterion for classifying studies in this section is that the results had to show significant psi-hitting. There was a natural break between these studies and those reviewed in the following section in that psi-coefficients, measures of effect per trial, tended to run below .05 here, while they ran much higher in the studies of talented subjects. The psi-coefficient (Timm, 1973) is a measure of the proportion of trials in which ESP is correctly used. Since it is independent of the number of choices of ESP targets, it allows comparison of different studies and will be used descriptively later. For ESP hitting, the psi-coefficient is given by the formula

$$\psi = \frac{H - np}{nq}$$

where H is the observed number of hits, n is the number of trials in the experiment, p is the probability of a hit, and q=1-p. The numerator is thus the observed number of hits (H) minus the number of hits that would be expected by chance alone (np), or the number of "true" hits, those due to ESP. The denominator (nq) is the proportion of trials in which there was an opportunity for ESP to manifest, viz., the total number of trials minus the proportion in which we expect hits by chance alone. The psi-coefficient (for hitting) ranges from zero (no more hits than expected by chance) to +1, a hit on every trial.

Note that the psi-coefficient does not reflect the difficulty of the ESP task: using ESP 10 percent of the time on a ten-choice task clearly calls for a more difficult discrimination than using it 10 percent of the time on a two-choice task.

The expectation from the learning theory application for mildly talented subjects is that the feedback should stabilize performance (eliminate declines) for short- to moderate-length experiments and perhaps allow some (presumably highly motivated) subjects to show some learning.

Mercer (1967) ran 20 subjects for 14 sessions each of 20 trials each, on a binary guessing test. Subjects given immediate feedback showed significantly more hits than chance (P < .0006), while those not receiving immediate feedback scored at chance. No details are available in the brief abstract reporting this study.

Schmidt (1970) designed a four-choice electronic ESP testing machine. Subjects tried to push the button which corresponded to the target lamp that would be selected next (a precognition study). The correct lamp immediately lit, providing feedback, although Schmidt did not consider feedback an important variable. In two precognition studies (Schmidt, 1969a), with four subjects who were preselected to show mild ESP ability, overall scoring for precognition was quite significant (P < 10⁻⁸ in each study). No analysis for the slopes of performance curves was reported, but in a later report on the same study (Schmidt, 1969c) Schmidt comments that scoring was "fairly steady," implying neither a consistent increase nor a decline for any subjects. It is of particular interest to note that subjects carried out more than 16,000 trials each in the first study, and more than 4,000 trials each in the second study. Since two of the three subjects in the second study also participated in the first one, "fairly steady" performance over more than 20,000 trials is remarkable, given the near universality of decline effects in studies without immediate feedback. In terms of actual magnitudes, these subjects were rather steadily scoring 26 percent to 27 percent hits rather than the 25 percent expected by chance.

In another study Schmidt (1969b) modified his apparatus to use targets already punched on paper tape, so they existed in present time and allowed for clairvoyance. Again subjects were preselected to have mild ESP ability; one had participated in the earlier (Schmidt, 1969a) study. Significant ESP ($P < 10^{-6}$) for the group was shown over a total of 15,000 trials. No data on performance slopes were presented.

Haraldsson (1970) used a slightly modified version of the Schmidt machine to try to show that subjects could score above chance (show precognition) on it, to test a method of selecting for mildly talented subjects, and to compare full feedback of results with partial feedback of results. The Schmidt machine was modified so that for full feedback condition a buzzer sounded when hits were made, in addition to the correct target lamp lighting so the subject could see it; for partial feedback condition the lamps were disconnected but the buzzer sounded, so the subject knew whether he was right or wrong but not what the correct target was if he was wrong.

In his selection study 74 subjects did 10 runs of 100 trials each, with the conditions alternating with each run between full and partial feedback. For the 740 runs overall there was a non-significant deviation below chance and no difference between the full and partial feedback conditions.

Individual subjects were allowed to go on to Haraldsson's main study if they scored suggestively above chance (psi-coefficients of about .02 or higher). Eleven subjects qualified and went on to the main series, where they did variable numbers of runs until the preset goal of 100 runs for the total group was met. (Haraldsson introduced a further selection procedure of dropping subjects who started to show negative scoring, but later further tested these subjects anyway and found only small differences, so we can ignore this procedure.) Scores were significantly above chance ($P < .002$) for the full feedback condition in the main study, but less significant for the partial feedback condition $(P < .04)$, although the formal difference between the two conditions was not significant. No slope data on performances over time are presented. Haraldsson noted that some of his better subjects preferred the partial feedback condition, for in lacking information about exactly what the missed target had been, they were less caught up in trying to figure out "patterns" in the target sequences.

Lewis and Schmeidler (1971) carried out a quite complex study of purposeful and non-purposeful ESP calls in the context of a biofeedback study for training alpha rhythm control. Extracting data immediately relevant to feedback, they used a four-choice machine of the Schmidt type with partial feedback: a red light came on for hits only. In two sessions, while hooked up for EEG recording, 14 unselected subjects each did a pre-test for precognition on the machine, had a free practice period, and then did a post-test. Partial feedback was provided throughout.

Pre-test precognition scores were insignificantly higher than chance, while the post-test scores were significantly above chance $(P = .02)$, but the difference was not statistically significant. There were significantly more hits when the subjects showed more alpha rhythm than usual. This study provides interesting hints for integrating biofeedback control of physiology and learning ESP.

Honorton (1971b) used a binary-choice precognition testing machine of the Schmidt type with a subject, M.B., who had many types of personal ESP experiences and was known as a "sensitive." Judging from his actual performance, I would classify him as mildly talented for this type of study (psi-coefficient = .02). Immediate feedback was provided by the correct lamp instantly lighting. M.B. worked in 16 trial runs, 10 runs to a set, and 12 sets per session, for a total of 1,920 trials per session. His overall score for eight sessions (total of 15,360 trials) was significantly above chance $(P = .002)$. The overall slope of his performance curve across sessions is positive, but not statistically significant. After an initial mean run score of 8.40 in his first session (8.00 expected by chance), he fell to chance in the second session, but thereafter showed a quite steady, mild rise until he regained his original scoring level by the eighth session. Is this learning or relearning? Honorton also found significant decline effects within each *set* when M.B. was trying to hit the target. For a subset of runs where M.B. deliberately tried to miss (a procedure he strongly disliked), there was a significant increase in hitting within the sets. Thus we have short-term variations imposed upon an overall increase in performance.

Schmidt and Pantas (1972) tested a number of groups of un-selected subjects on Schmidt's four-choice precognition machine, with full and immediate feedback from the correct target lamp lighting. In their first experiment, subjects deliberately tried to miss, and as soon as a subject hit, his place was taken by the next subject in the group. However, Schmidt and Pantas manipulated the psychological atmosphere of the testing conditions so they expected psi-hitting, even though the subjects were trying to miss. A total of 500 trials, set in advance, was carried out. The results were significantly above chance (P < .01), and there was a slight increase in scoring rate (28.4 percent to 29.2 percent) from the first to the second half of the experiment, although it was not statistically significant.

The second part of the Schmidt and Pantas study involved a highly talented subject and will be reported on later.

This study is also of great methodological significance, for in another series Schmidt and Pantas modified the internal circuitry of the test machine so that it required psychokinetic action on the generator to score above chance. Subjects still believed they were trying to *predict*, not knowing of the modification, but they significantly *influenced* the machine. Thus subjects who believe they are trying to use some form of ESP may alter the behavior of a random number generator by unconsciously using psychokinesis.

Honorton (1970; 1971a) and McCallam and Honorton (1973) carried out three studies which further support the application of learning theory to ESP performance. Honorton's second study was a replication of the first, and the McCallam and Honorton study extended and replicated the first two. The basic design was to have 20 subjects, divided into experimental and control groups of 10 each, tested individually. There was immediate feedback of results in the experimental group and *false* feedback in the control group.

Initially each subject guessed at targets in six standard closed decks of Zener cards (five each of five symbols), and also indicated when he felt particularly confident about the correctness of a call. Such "confidence calls" have often been evaluated separately from total calls in parapsychological research and are frequently associated with a higher hitting rate. The randomized test cards were left enclosed in their boxes for the test procedure, a DT (down through) clairvoyance procedure, and there was no feedback. The experimental group then had immediate feedback runs on three more decks: whenever the subject was correct, the experimenter immediately called out "Right!" This constituted partial feedback of information. The control group had an apparently similar (to them) session of three feedback runs, except that the experimenter called "Right!" when the subject's response was actually incorrect, a false feedback condition. The experimenter called "Right" about the same number of times in each condition. Both groups then went on to three more DT clairvoyance runs, again making confidence calls, as in the pre-feedback condition.

In the two Honorton studies this false feedback condition was used, while in the McCallam and Honorton study a no-feedback condition was used for the control group.

In all three studies, there was a significant increase in the proportion of *correct* confidence calls, so subjects were learning something about the internal feelings that go with correct ESP performance. Further, in the first and third studies, the feedback group showed significant ESP hitting on their total scores as well as significant increases on their confidence calls following the feedback condition, even though their scoring had not differed significantly from chance before the training. Note also that, as would be expected from the learning theory application, subjects in the false feedback group showed a tendency, although it was not statistically significant, to make *lower* overall ESP scores and a *lower* proportion of correct confidence calls after the false feedback condition.

The McCallam and Honorton study found a result which, at first glance, seems incongruous with the learning theory application. They ran two other groups who received six and nine feedback runs, respectively. We would expect that more training would produce an even greater effect, but the feedback training did not produce any effect at all on the post-feedback DT clairvoyance runs in these other two groups. Why? My speculation is that the more extended training intensified a flaw in Honorton's and McCallam's training procedure, viz., that they used closed decks (five of each of five symbols) for the feedback conditions. It has long been known that you cannot legitimately *test* for ESP when giving immediate feedback with closed decks. By keeping track (consciously or unconsciously) of what has already turned up, the subject can optimize his guesses near the end, i.e., if he knows all five stars have already come up he will no longer guess star, and thus will increase his hit probability on the remaining cards. I suspect that in the more extended training with closed decks, McCallam's and Honorton's subjects began improving their memories, not their ESP abilities. This probably didn't happen much in the short (three run) training groups because of the subjects' focus on the ESP task, but it would have become the winning strategy in the longer training.

Kreiman and Ivnisky (1973) replicated Honorton's first two studies with a larger group, and while they did not find an increase in the proportion of correct confidence calls, as had Honorton, they did find a significant increase in overall ESP performance after the feedback training, as Honorton (1970) and McCallam and Honorton (1973) found.

Dagle (1968), in a master's thesis (abstracted in Dagle & Puryear, 1969), reported on three studies utilizing immediate feedback. Subjects worked at a binary-choice GESP (General Extra-Sensory Perception) task, the experimenter trying to "send" the correct button to push from another room. Pushing the response button gave immediate feedback. Student subjects were preselected on a card test and divided into those who scored above and below chance, a very crude division into possibly mildly talented and non-talented subjects. For both groups, there was an increase in scoring when a block of non-feedback trials was followed by a block of feedback trials; this was true for all six subjects in the mildly talented group and was statistically significant. When feedback trials came first, the level of scoring was roughly maintained in the subsequent non-feedback trials.

Unfortunately, Dagle used a closed deck in this first study, a deck with a fixed number of each of the alternative cards. Since this fact was known to the subjects, it is possible that some of them simply kept track of what targets had already been used and modified their guessing strategy accordingly, thus raising their scores by non-paranormal means. Use of the same target deck for all subjects also introduced the possibility of a stacking effect, which could inflate scoring levels by 10 percent or more.[4] The fact that the mildly talented subjects (by prior, non-feedback ESP card guessing test criteria) showed learning and the non-talented ones did not argues against this interpretation, but since we cannot be sure, Dagle's first study must be considered tentative.

Dagle carried out a second study similar to the first, but with subjects making confidence ratings of each call by moving a lever. Three of the six subjects showed individually significant results for ESP (assuming we are not dealing with a closed deck again, an item not specified in Dagle's thesis), although the results were not related to confidence ratings. The procedure inadvertently introduced fairly long delays between a subject's decision and his response, however, so it is not clear whether to consider this *immediate* feedback or not.[5]

In a brief third study, Dagle had two subjects carry out seven and six runs, respectively, with immediate feedback. Both showed individually significant scoring for ESP. One showed a highly positive slope (+2.085), although this resulted mainly from a very low score on the first run, and the other a steady performance. Again, this study is flawed by the use of closed target decks.

Fouts (1973) reported two studies testing the effects of almost immediate feedback on ESP. In the first, two college student subjects, selected only because they believed in ESP and were friends, carried out a four-choice GESP task, the woman always acting as sender and the man always acting as receiver. A pass option was provided when the receiver did not want to guess. In a 100-trial (including passes) baseline period with no feedback, this team showed only chance results (24.7 percent hits when 25 percent was expected by chance). Relatively immediate feedback (I guess one to three seconds, depending on how fast Fouts, the experimenter, operated the apparatus) on both target and response was then given to both sender and receiver. The 528 trials (including an unreported number of passes) with feedback averaged 31.5 percent correct hits ($P = 8x10^{-4}$).[6] Looking at the data in the feedback condition in 48 trial blocks (including passes), there seemed to be quite steady improvement through the first five blocks (25.5 percent, 33.3 percent, 39.2 percent, 36.4 percent, and 43.6 percent hits, respectively), but then a falling off to lower performance levels in the rest of the experiment. Fouts remarks that the subjects lost interest as the experiment went on and had to be coaxed to continue.

Unfortunately this study is flawed, as neither the number of trials per session nor the total number of trials for the experiment was fixed in advance, so optional stopping by the subjects that took advantage of chance fluctuations is possible. Thus I consider these results to be consistent with the learning theory application, but they should not carry undue weight.

In his second study, Fouts ran a class of 53 students simultaneously on a three-choice GESP task, again with a pass option. When a signal light at the front of the room came on, each student tried to guess what the sender in another room was concentrating on, and then marked his or her answer down on an individual answer sheet. Twenty-four non-feedback trials at the start constituted a baseline series, followed by 96 trials in which the class instructor gave feedback on the correct target at the end of each 10-second trial period. Unfortunately this gave students the opportunity to write down their answers *after* the feedback had been given. While Fouts asked students if they had done this on any trials, and consequently eliminated from further analyses the results of 12 subjects who replied affirmatively, we cannot be sure that this might not have happened occasionally with other subjects, so the results of this second study can also be considered only tentative. The study results are also open to distortion by the stacking effect, discussed earlier, since all subjects were guessing at the same target order; thus the significance levels may be artifactually inflated.

Fouts reported there were 31.6 percent hits in the baseline period, a non-significant negative deviation from the chance expectancy of

33.33 percent hits. For the feedback condition there were 35.4 percent hits (P = .004). Looking at the data in 12-trial blocks, the findings are peculiar. There was an immediate jump to 41 percent hits in the first feedback block, but lower performance, with some variability, after that, so the slope of the group's performance curve does not differ significantly from zero. Feedback may have aided ESP performance and stabilized it but did not produce learning for the group. Individual data were not reported.

Sandford and Keil (1975) carried out a preliminary experiment with a single subject, one of the experimenters (Sandford). They used a four-choice task of guessing which light on a panel had been selected as target by the experimenter in another room, a GESP setup. This was a partial feedback setup: pressing the correct response button turned out the ready light, thus providing immediate feedback, but pressing an incorrect response button did not indicate what the target had been. The subject carried out 600 trials in 10 sessions, half the sessions in his ordinary state, half of them after self-induction of a state of deep relaxation. Overall ESP results for the 600 trials of the combined conditions did not differ significantly from chance, although there was a suggestive (P = .11) positive performance slope. The normal-state condition by itself showed significant ESP hitting (P < .05), while the relaxed-state scores were at chance. Slope data are not presented separately for the two conditions. Hand recording of data by the experimenter also allows the possibility of recording errors.

Targ, Cole, and Puthoff (1974) have conducted four separate studies, the most extensive to date, of the possibilities of learning ESP. Each study used the Aquarius Model 100 ESP Trainer (described in chapter 4), with or without automatic data recording equipment. This is a four-choice electronic machine with instant feedback. Their Phase 0 pilot study resulted in two subjects whose hit scores and positive slopes of increasing performance were individually significant. One subject (A-1), a child, showed a mean score of 26.06 hits per 100 trials when 25 would be expected by chance (P = .008), but while the increase in slope of this curve was statistically significant (P = 10^{-6}), the actual magnitude of the slope was very low. The slope was .07, meaning that it required about 15 runs of 100 trials each to add one extra ESP hit to the score. The second subject's scores showed much more ESP (a mean of 30.5 instead of 25) and a quite positive slope (slope = .714 over 1,400 trials, a remarkable increase of about three-quarters of an ESP hit for every 100 trials). His psi-coefficient is high enough (.07) to consider him with the highly talented subjects. Unfortunately, this subject, a scientist, recorded his own data, and the first subject's data were reported by his father. Since it is a general rule in parapsychological research never to allow subjects *any* opportunity to make recording errors or to cheat, these results must be considered tentative.[7]

In the Targ et al. Phase I study, 145 subjects participated in at least five 15- to 20-minute sessions each on the Aquarius machine. Data were machine recorded. The total number of hits for the group as a whole was almost exactly what one would expect by chance, so, as a group, no ESP was shown. Nine of the 145 subjects showed positive learning slopes that were statistically significant at the .05 level or better, and 11 showed mean scores significant at the .05 level or better. Targ et al. report that the exact binomial probability of their observed, significant positive slopes occurring by chance is 3×10^{-3}. Curiously, none of the subjects who showed significantly positive slopes showed a significant number of hits above chance expectation. Thus subjects showing significantly positive slopes must have had many below chance scores at the beginning of their performance.

At first glance it is tempting to view this as regression to the mean, simple chance variation, but this is not a legitimate interpretation because there were no significantly negative slopes; yet there should have been about as many as there were significantly positive slopes if we were dealing only with regression to the mean. Apparently we have ESP-missing here. As discussed in the following chapter, such ESP-missing greatly complicates the simple application of learning theory. Phase I results provide some support for the learning hypothesis, since there were no significantly negative slopes, but the amount of ESP was very small.

Targ et al. felt that unpleasant experimental conditions, such as the noise of the automatic data recording printer on the Aquarius machine, were at least partly responsible for poor scoring in Phase I, so their Phase II experiment was done under better conditions—in a more pleasant room, from which the noisy printer was removed (it was still connected to the machine but was recording remotely). Twelve subjects participated, all selected as either having shown mean scores significantly above chance or having significantly positive slopes in Phase 0, Phase I, or some informal work. Subjects carried out 1,000–6,000 trials each. Unfortunately, no subjects showed mean hits significantly different from chance in Phase II, and no subjects showed significantly positive slopes. This is inconsistent with the predictions of the learning theory application for at least two of the subjects (A-2 and A-3) showed a great deal of ESP in earlier studies (each scored more hits than chance with a significance at the 10^{-6} level). Whether this argues against learning theory or may be due to the change in conditions of the Phase II study is unknown. Targ et al. feel that the still complex conditions of Phase II inhibited the subjects' performance.

In their final study, Phase III, Targ et al. ran eight subjects, again selected on the basis of significantly positive slopes or significantly high mean scoring in the earlier phases. Conditions were now more informal, with the experimenter remaining in the room to read the data from the machine but the automatic recording removed, to dispel any inhibiting effect on the subjects. Seven of the eight subjects showed no significant results in terms of either number of hits or slopes. A-3, the only subject who had shown extremely significant results in Phase I ($P = 10^{-6}$), did recover his ESP abilities. He scored an average of 29.57 when 25 was expected by chance over 2,800 trials ($P = 10^{-6}$). However, his slope, while slightly positive (slope $= +.135$), was not significantly different from chance.

Two of the Targ et al. studies, Phases II and III, allowed me to examine the relationship between mean ESP scoring rate and the slopes of the curves obtained under conditions of immediate feedback. In Phase II, where two subjects showed significantly negative scores, the correlation is -.29, which does not begin to approach statistical significance. But, since the range of ESP scoring was extremely limited, perhaps with no real ESP in the experiment at all (overall results were not significant), and since all the obtained slopes were essentially zero (the largest was -.0004), we cannot expect to see any relationship here.

The Phase III results are presented for seven subjects, whose overall and individual results showed no significant deviations from chance (for either mean score or slope), and separately for an outstanding psi-hitter. For the seven subjects, the correlation is +.91 between mean ESP score and slope (P < .005). This high correlation is achieved primarily because the largest negative slope by far was associated with the lowest-scoring subject. If the high-scoring subject's scored trials (not his practice runs) are added into the group of seven, the correlation becomes +.68 (P < .05). These results support my prediction from learning theory, though the range of ESP scoring is even more restricted than in Phase II. The slopes of subjects in Phase III show a much wider range, however.

To summarize the Targ, Cole, and Puthoff experiments, most of their subjects showed no ESP, and of those who did, few were able to hold up in futher studies. The same is true for those who showed significantly positive slopes (even though their overall ESP score was not significant). One subject out of 147 was able to show consistently good ESP results, and, in the two studies in which he scored significantly (Phase I and Phase III), his slope, although positive, was not statistically significant, suggesting he was able to hold up in his ESP performance without extinguishing it, but not showing clear-cut learning.

Studies with Highly Talented Subjects

Although I have no a priori way of predicting the talent threshold, above which the learning process should predominate over the extinction inherent in success by chance, the studies reviewed in this section involve subjects who were outstandingly more successful than subjects in other studies. These subjects were often able to demonstrate ESP by showing statistically significant scoring in a single test. We shall look at talent levels more precisely in chapter 6.

The first study to note here was by Ojha (1964). Although it was published in 1964, completely independently of my own formulation of the learning theory application, I did not learn of it until 1974. Ojha, working from a psychological approach dealing with *knowledge of results* (feedback), hypothesized that complete knowledge (what the target was) of results in a guessing situation would give higher scores than partial knowledge (right or wrong), and partial knowledge would be better than no knowledge. He used a closed deck of 100 cards, with the numbers one, two, three, and four randomly assigned, 25 of each kind. Six groups of five individuals each received various degrees of immediate knowledge of results. The results fitted the hypothesis. *Assuming*, as Ojha did, that 25 out of 100 would be expected correct by chance, the group having complete knowledge of results had a mean of 32.6 correct, the group having partial knowledge of the results had a mean of 29.4, and the group with no knowledge of results had a mean of 24.6, highly significant differences.

Unfortunately, Ojha's study is seriously flawed from the parapsychological point of view because he used a closed deck. It is not clear whether he told his subjects that there was an equal frequency of each target card, but even if he did not explicitly tell them so, this would be a possible inference on their part. Thus, if many of a particular number had already turned up (known to the subjects through the feedback), the subjects would be less likely to call that number in the future and thereby would elevate their scores without recourse to ESP. It is essentially the same procedure any good card player uses of keeping track of what's been played in order to improve his ability to guess what might still be concealed in other players' hands. Because of this possible drawback, Ojha's study can be seen only as tentatively supporting the learning theory.

Targ and Hurt (1972) developed a fully automated, four-choice machine similar to ESPATESTER (see appendix 2). They report on 12 subjects. As in the other studies reviewed, there was no pre-selection for ESP ability, only for interest in working with the machine. One child subject showed clear ESP scoring on the task of clairvoyantly perceiving the state of the machine. In a total series of 64 runs of 24 trials each, she made an average of 8.6 hits per run, with a probability of approximately 10^{-15}. She showed clear improvement over her trials, learning to score at very high levels of significance on individual runs. At the 65th run, the machine was rewired to a precognition mode without informing the subject, i.e., the target was not generated until two-tenths of a second *after* the subject's guess. The subject at first said she no longer felt anything and was just guessing; she scored at chance. However, in the course of 28 runs her performance increased to a level approaching her scores in the clairvoyance tests: in her first 4 runs, for example, she obtained 19 hits (when 24 would be expected by chance), and in her last 4 runs she made 38 hits. The slope of the fitted regression line was .56 (P < .01), indicating an average gain of about one ESP hit in every 8 runs (192 trials). This was clear evidence of learning.

Targ's and Hurt's study has a drawback, however, in that it is not clear from their report whether either experimenter actually observed the subject's performance or not, even though presumably the machine did not allow for fraud.[8]

Kelly and Kanthamani (1972) describe a case of ESP learning under conditions of immediate feedback, although they do not conceptualize the task that way. A gifted subject, B.D., worked on a new Schmidt four-choice precognition testing machine (Schmidt & Pantas, 1972), where he had to press a button to indicate which lamp would be selected next by a random number generator. The machine gave immediate and complete feedback as the selected lamp lit, and also emitted a single auditory click on misses and a double click on hits. His initial performance, under tight conditions, was extremely significant (180 hits in 508 trials when 127 are expected by chance, P < 10^{-7}). When a mechanical punch was connected to the machine to automatically record data, however, he lost most of his ability, for psychological reasons not specified by Kelly and Kanthamani. He dropped from a level of about 33.3 percent to 27 percent correct. After a period of anger at the machine and frustration at his inability to score, B.D. determined to relearn his ability in spite of the mechanical punch. In eight days of intense, concentrated practice, with the machine providing immediate feedback, he steadily raised his scoring level from 27 percent back up to 30.8 percent, a clear case of learning (or perhaps *re*learning, depending on the importance of the change made by the connection of the punch).

Kanthamani and Kelly (1974) performed another experiment with their exceptional subject, B.D., where he was shown a black folder containing a single playing card and given almost immediate feedback on his call; the experimenter wrote down the call before pulling the card from the folder, so there was a delay of about one second.

B.D. had participated in an earlier experiment of this type with Irvin Child and had scored significantly ($P < .01$ on suit hits), but not at a level to match his outstanding performance on a variety of other ESP tests.

In the Kanthamani and Kelly experiment, usually one run of 52 trials composed a session, with a break about halfway through. The target cards were drawn from a large deck of 10 full decks, an effective open deck, so knowledge of calls would not significantly alter the probabilities of unused, upcoming targets. B.D. felt that the quick feedback was important for him to learn to do well in this task, although for some trials he asked not to be given feedback, usually when he felt very "hot" and sure of success.

There were four experimental series, the first two of 13 runs each and the second two of 10 runs each. Scoring was by an exact method, initially proposed by Fisher, that considers nine classes of responses, as well as an overall response. The overall Fisher z-score was not significant for the first series, although there were significantly more number-only hits than would be expected by chance. The overall Fisher z-score was extremely high for the second series ($z = 11.25$), primarily from an excessive number of exact (suit and number) hits. The overall scoring level fell to $z = 5.39$ and $z = 5.18$ in the third and fourth series, still well above chance expectation, again with most of the significance being contributed by an excess of exact hits.

While the Fisher method of analysis of this data is very precise, it does not convey a clear impression of actual scoring. If we consider that B.D. was trying for exact hits (suit and number), the probability of this for one run is 1/52, or 1.92 percent. For the four series, B.D.'s mean run scores for exact hits were 2.5 percent, 8.9 percent, 5.6 percent, and 6.2 percent.

Thus B.D. seems to have learned to some degree in the first

series, pushed the learning process about as far as he could go in the second series, and dropped to a steady but still extremely significant scoring rate in the third and fourth series, perhaps because they did not continue to constitute a challenge.

Kanthamani and Kelly compare scoring on the feedback and non-feedback trials, and find it much higher on the non-feedback trials. This comparison is irrelevant to the question of whether feedback can allow subjects to increase their ESP performance, however, for B.D. tended to request non-feedback trials at times when he felt "hot," i.e., when he felt confident (as the result of the feedback training preceding these non-feedback trials?).

Schmidt and Pantas (1972), in the second part of their study, performed a separate experiment on one of the authors, Lee Pantas, who had shown unusually high ability in self-testing on the Schmidt machine. He carried out 500 trials at the rate of 25 trials per session, one session per day, working quite slowly and practicing Zen meditation for about 20 minutes just before each session. He scored well above chance ($P \approx 5 \times 10^{-5}$), although no data are presented on the slope of his performance curve. He also scored well in attempting to psychokinetically influence the machine.

With highly talented subjects, then, we see steady and highly significant performance and/or clear increases, learning, of ESP ability. We shall consider these differences among subjects at different talent levels more precisely in chapter 6.

3   A Pilot Study:
Psi-Missing and Fear of Psi

 In the spring quarter of 1972 the students in a small class in experimental psychology I was teaching became interested in working with the idea of teaching ESP ability through the application of feedback, so an informal pilot study was carried out. Using the Ten-Choice Trainer (TCT), described in detail in chapter 4, 10 student subjects (not class members) carried out anywhere from 60 to 1,720 trials, in runs of from 10 to 40 trials each. On each trial the subject had to guess which of 10 unlit lamps had been selected as target, while the experimenter, located in another room, was concentrating on telepathically sending it. The subjects were informally selected, mainly on the basis of their interest in participating, plus any sort of feeling by individual experimenters that they might have ESP abilities. While the experimental conditions were quite tight in terms of eliminating any factors but ESP to account for scoring, they were otherwise quite informal. Run length, for example, varied from 10 to 40 trials per run, and the total number of sessions was not fixed ahead of time but was determined by how long each subject/experimenter team wanted to work together.[1]

For the group as a whole, the number of hits is not significantly different from chance (551 hits where 532.5 would be expected). Inspection of the individual data, however, reveals that one subject scored exceptionally well: she (PS1) made 98 hits where 42.5 would

I gratefully acknowledge the assistance of my students, Jim Guthrie, Hal McMillan, and Mark Warren, and especially of my colleague and assistant, Lois Dick, who acted as experimenters.

be expected by chance, over double chance expectation ($P < 2 \times 10^{-18}$, 2-tailed). Yet her highly significant scoring was canceled out in the group results because of other subjects who scored below chance. Two of these latter subjects scored suggestively and significantly below chance (PS3 and PS9). A third below-chance subject, while not reaching statistical significance (PS8), had over four times as many trials as our high scorer, so his and the other two significantly negative subjects' scores canceled out the effect of our high scorer in the group average.

TABLE 1   Pilot Study Results by Subject, TCT[a]

Subject	Total Trials	Run Length	Hits/ Expected	P (2-tailed)	Overall Slope
PS1	425	varied	98/42.5	2×10^{-18}	-.05[b]
PS4	400	40	47/40	ns	.22
PS5	240	40	29/24	ns	-.49
PS7	280	40	31/28	ns	.54
PS10	260	varied	28/26	ns	-.21[b]
PS6	560	40	55/56	ns	-.00
PS8	1,720	40	157/172	ns	-.00
PS2	60	20	3/6	ns	-.50
PS3	300	varied	20/30	.06	-.25[b]
PS9	1,080	40	83/108	.01	.02
Total of 10 subjects	5,325	. . . . . .	551/532.5	ns	-.07

[a]Note that in the original Parapsychology Foundation monograph I inadvertently used one-tailed rather than two-tailed probabilities, and the slope values of subjects PS8 and PS3 were mistakenly interchanged in the table.

[b]Because these subjects varied the length of their runs, z-scores were used in calculating slopes, and the units for measuring these slopes are thus a unit normal distribution with a mean of zero and a standard deviation of one.

None of the slopes of the regression lines is significantly different from zero at even the .05 level of significance. As will be seen later, in looking at performance curves of individual subjects, the slopes of fitted (straight) regression lines are often not a good representative way of describing the actual performance. As would be predicted by learning theory, there is a positive correlation between mean psi-hitting and the slopes, but this correlation ($r = +.10$) is not statistically significant.

Individual Performance

The performance of our high-scoring psi-hitter is worth examining in detail. It is graphed in figure 1. Because she varied her run length, the z-score of each run rather than the raw score is plotted.

A striking feature of this graph is the extreme variability. Her observed variance is more than four times that expected by chance ($P \ll .001$). She varied from runs at chance (1 hit/10 trials) or (non-significantly) below chance to runs that were significant at less than the 10^{-7} level: these highest two runs each showed scores of 6 hits in 10 trials, roughly indicating ESP was being used on half rather that one-tenth of her responses.

The second important feature of the graph is the below-chance scores in the last session, runs 18 and 19. She had done extremely well in the previous session, but had "freaked out" at the end of it. She cried hysterically for a long period and did not want to participate any further in the study. She would not explain why, and she would not be comforted. Because of her extreme ESP success we did not want her to quit, and we later arranged, after considerable resistance on her part, for another session. This is the final session shown, where she scored below chance in two runs (3 hits in 40 trials and 0 hits in 10 trials). She made her determination not to participate further quite clear!

My hypothesis to explain this unusual behavior and scoring, judging from what the experimenter, Lois Dick, knew of her, as well as general considerations about ESP, is as follows. Up to a certain level of ESP scoring, unique for each individual, successful scoring can be dealt with as an *intellectually* interesting phenomenon. It's very statistical and abstract. Many people, however, have an unconscious or partially conscious fear of ESP and resistance to it. Ordinarily, people are never confronted with *obvious* instances of ESP, so they may either ignore it entirely or only play with it intellectually. It's not really *real*. Our subject apparently had some deep-seated fears of ESP, however, and her continually increasing success (the slope of her performance curve is .08 through run 17, which, while not statistically significant, is positive) finally forced her to confront, or at least activated her *fear* of confronting, the

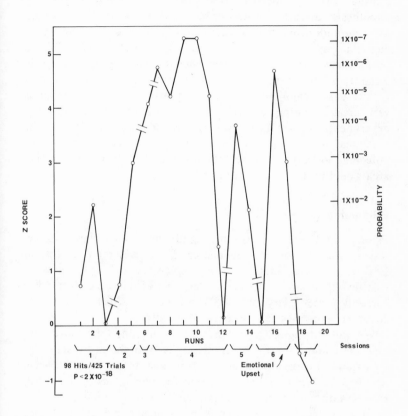

Fɪɢ. 1.   Performance of pilot study subject PS1

experiential, emotional reality of ESP, and this triggered the emotional outburst. The high variability in scoring before this may also have been reflecting her fear and ambivalence about ESP. Her resolution of this conflict was to suppress her ESP abilities, both by quitting the experiment so they could not be further trained and by doing very poorly when we prevailed upon her to come back for another session.

I shall formalize this as a further prediction to add to the learning hypothesis: Given that a subject has sufficient ESP ability to show learning under conditions of immediate feedback, if he has semi-conscious or unconscious fears of and resistance to ESP, a performance level will be reached where he will have to confront in some form this non-conscious fear and resistance. This may manifest as an emotional outburst, as quitting the experiment, or as very erratic scoring, possibly culminating in psi-missing. The experimenter's and subject's willingness and ability to deal with the emotional bases of the conflict will have a great effect on the outcome. Some type of psychotherapy oriented toward the conflict area would probably be useful.

Psi-missing

Psi-missing, where subjects score significantly below chance expectation, is a well-known phenomenon. It involves the operation of ESP as much as does psi-hitting, since the only way to score significantly below chance is for some part of the subject's mind to correctly perceive targets by ESP and then so affect the subject's conscious responses as to insure wrong calls.

We can distinguish two kinds of psi-missing: motivated and malfunctioning. Motivated psi-missing is exemplified by Schmeidler's classical experiments on the sheep-goat effect (Schmeidler & McConnell, 1958). Subjects who, before being tested for ESP, express a disbelief in it (the goats), tend to score significantly below chance compared to subjects who express a belief in ESP (the sheep). These motivated goats apparently function under the academic paradigm that poor performance on a test means you know little, and the poorer your performance the less you know, so scoring as low as possible seems to be a validation of their belief system that there is no ESP. Presumably they do not understand the statistical principles that make very low scoring as significant as very high scoring.

Malfunctioning psi-missing would simply imply that a subject can somehow get the ESP "receptor mechanism" operating by trying but that there is a malfunctioning process somewhere between the receptor mechanism and his actual calls that creates errors. However, there is no motivated need to score low; it is simply malfunctioning of the whole system that is involved.

What would happen to psi-missers put into an immediate feedback ESP training situation with instructions to improve their performance? For the malfunctioning psi-misser, we would probably see exceptionally high variability of scoring, for the feedback would allow him to start to affect the ESP-guessing system, crudely at first, then more precisely. Thus the malfunctioning psi-misser might be able to correct the malfunctioning eventually, and so begin to learn after initial variability.

Prediction of the performance of the motivated psi-misser put into an immediate feedback ESP training situation is more difficult. Here we are dealing not just with the mechanics of learning but with unconscious motivation, cognitive dissonance, and styles of resolving conflict. If the need to miss dominated performance, for example, and the subject got progressively *worse*, he would realize that he was not living up to his conscious commitment to the instructions to try to get better, and/or he would suspect he was using ESP. I could predict great variability of scores, but cannot be more specific at this time.

The performance of the most outstanding psi-misser in the pilot study, PS9, is plotted in figure 2. She scored an average of 3.07 hits per run of 40, when 4 would be expected by chance ($P = .01$).

Was she a motivated psi-misser, or a malfunctioning psi-misser? We cannot tell from the performance curve alone. The extreme variability, mainly in the first 14 runs, may reflect an erratically malfunctioning process (or processes) involved in ESP and calling, or it might reflect swings due to emotional ambivalence as some learning began. If we fitted a regression line to these first 14 runs it would have an essentially zero slope of $+.08$, but then we have a much less variable performance curve that shows a significantly ($P < .05$) positive slope of $+.18$ Was the subject's motivated psi-missing resolved by run 14, so that she no longer needed to miss and could now allow herself to learn, or had she finally started to learn to stabilize and control her malfunctioning psi processes? In cases like this, we need additional psychological information about belief systems and motives to make these distinctions.

In general, then, the pilot study found one subject showing

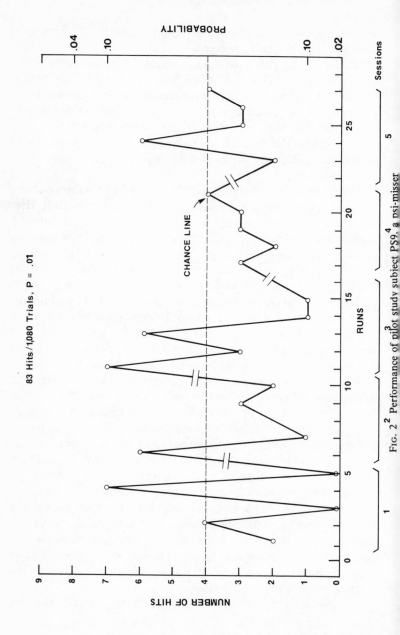

FIG. 2 Performance of pilot study subject PS9, a psi-misser

significant psi-hitting, and perhaps two showing significant psi-missing. It demonstrated how the role of resistance to ESP must be considered in addition to straightforward considerations from learning theory.

4 A Three-Stage Study in Training ESP Ability

with Dana J. Redington

In the fall of 1973 I was scheduled to teach a small class on experimental psychology. I believed that the best way to learn how to do experiments is to do some rather than just read about them. I also believed that doing a parapsychological experiment would be an exceptionally valuable way of teaching this class, since methodological standards in parapsychology are generally higher than those in other areas of psychology. I asked my students if they would like to do a group experiment on ESP under my direction to see if we could produce learning in accordance with my theory. I made it clear that in return for this restriction on their freedom of choice as to the nature of the experiment they would get a much greater amount of enthusiastic attention from me than if they did something that I wasn't really interested in. The students agreed to this procedure. Indeed, as time went on they became very enthusiastic experimenters.

The author was responsible for the inception, overall direction, analysis, and writeup of this study; Dana J. Redington took a major role in directing day-to-day experimentation, computer analysis of data, and technical maintenance of the equipment.

I want to express my thanks to my students, Hector Aponte, Scott Archbold, Alan Croft, Bruce Frankel, Laurie Gates, Mark Glatt, David Kraus, Eric Larsen, Judi Norquist, Frank Odasz, Gaines Thomas, Ryan Unruh, Mark Watts, Wanda Welch, and Bruce Westlund, and my assistants, Neil Goodman and Irene Segrest, whose efforts made the Selection and Confirmation Studies possible. I especially want to thank the Parapsychology Foundation, Eileen Coly, President, for providing financial support for this research, and the Institute for the Study of Human Knowledge, which provided the administrative structure for the financial support.

Experimenter Characteristics

Since I strongly believe that the experimenter is very much a part of every experiment, it is necessary to say something about my relationship as principal investigator to the other experimenters and, later, about the relationship of the experimenters to the subjects. My relationship to the experimenters was bounded by the fact that I was a professor and they were students, with the constant pressure of grades in the background. I made it clear at the beginning of the class that I didn't like to give grades and was well aware of all their shortcomings, but that as long as everyone worked enthusiastically they would certainly get a B or an A, as my tests would not be difficult. The students were given the option—if this was not acceptable procedure, if they did not want to do a lot of work on the experiment—to drop out of the class. Since it was not a required class, the students had real choice in the matter.

In general, I acted in an open, friendly manner, and with a good deal of personal enthusiasm about the importance and significance of the experiment we were doing. This was balanced with exercises designed to stimulate the critical faculties of the student/experimenters about parapsychological matters, and a constant emphasis on the total honesty and highest methodological standards required for ESP work. I enthusiastically presented my 1966 theory that feedback would probably lead to learning, but also pointed out that it was not yet proved. Nevertheless, I deliberately created an atmosphere conveying that it was almost certainly true and that we would have the opportunity to confirm or deny it in an important way. We planned all the detailed steps of the experiment together, discussing a very wide variety of options, and had an excellent, cooperative relationship.

D. J. Redington was also a student in the class, which further helped in bridging any teacher-student gap.

Another important factor to note in understanding the relationships between the students in the class who became the experimenters and their later subjects is that we tried to get away from the typical "colonial paradigm" used in most psychological (and parapsychological) experiments, viz., a paradigm where the white sahib exploits the natives, where the all-knowing, high status experimenter manipulates the ignorant subjects for the benefit of himself and his peers. In order to allow the student/experimenters to personally understand how widespread this situation is, and to get a feel for its effects, I led them in an experiental exercise early in the class. This exercise, devised by Claudio Naranjo, is a controlled associations task where each person rapidly writes down a key word over and over for 15 minutes. Whenever an association pops into consciousness, it is written down, but then the repeated writing of the key word is immediately recommenced. Thus a cluster of associations to the key word develops that gives clues to personal feelings about it that would probably not surface from a more intellectual, "thinking about it" approach. The key word, for example, might be "science," and a section of the written responses might be "science, science, science, science, H-bomb, science, modern, science, science, science, manipulative, science, science . . . "

We did 15 minutes each of controlled associations to the words *science, experimenter,* and *subject.* Then we pooled the class's associations and found that from the students' own experiences there emerged a clear picture of science as often cold, antihuman, and exploitative, and of experimenters as authoritarian, manipulative, lying, unfeeling, etc., while subjects were one-down, exploited, depersonalized, interchangeable, rebellious, etc.

This exercise was very successful in bringing out personal feelings about the colonial paradigm in experimentation and one of its main consequences, viz., subjects deliberately doing poorly in experiments or covertly trying to sabotage them as the only way in which to express their resentment. Thus the effort, in our experimental procedure, to treat subjects as colleagues and to be warm and open with them sprang from a personal realization of the qualities and drawbacks of the usual colonial paradigm.

General Procedure

The general plan of the study we eventually put together is shown as a flow chart in figure 3. Given that we needed individuals who could already show some ESP in order for the reinforcement to be effective, as called for by the theory, we realized we would need an initial phase (hereafter called the Selection Study) to screen very large numbers of individuals and select only those who showed significant signs of ESP. Then we would need a second confirmatory phase (hereafter called the Confirmation Study) in which to confirm that the individuals we had actually selected did indeed have ESP, rather than having scored high only by chance, as is bound to happen in testing very large numbers of subjects. Subjects who did well in this Confirmation Study would go on to the third phase (hereafter referred to as the Training Study), where they would receive 20 runs of 25 trials each with immediate feedback, in an attempt to increase their ESP. We realized that 20 runs was probably much too short, but this was the compromise we had to make, given the reality of the academic quarter system and the time commitments of both experimenters and subjects.

We shall now consider each phase in detail.

Selection Study

The purpose of this first study was to find subjects who had demonstrable psychic ability. Since we considered such ability relatively rare, and our resources for screening subjects were limited, we decided to follow two procedures. The main procedure would be that of doing brief card guessing tests in large University of California, Davis, classes, and the minor procedure would be to individually test some people who, for one reason or another, the particular experimenter believed might have psychic ability.

For the main selection procedure, the experimenters worked in subgroups of three or four and carried out ESP card guessing tests in classes whose size ranged from 20 to 400. The two decks of target cards consisted of ordinary playing cards which had had all the face cards and all the numbered cards from six and up culled from them, i.e., each became a deck of 25 cards with five aces, five twos, five threes, five fours, and five fives. Each target deck was thoroughly randomized by hand immediately before the class testing. Subjects were instructed that only the number was the target and the suit could be disregarded.[1]

Having first obtained permission from the class instructor, the experimenters would come in 10 to 15 minutes before the end of the class. While one experimenter gave a very brief (two or three minutes) talk on ESP, the purpose of this study, and instructions for the test,

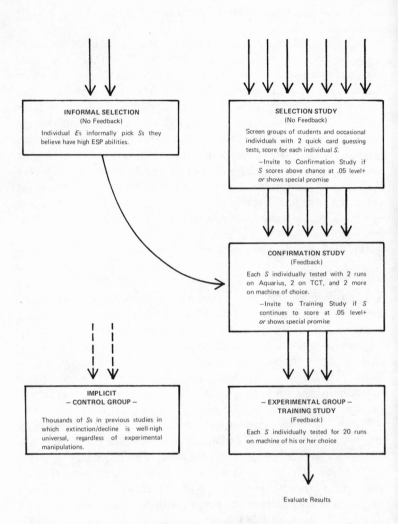

INFORMAL SELECTION
(No Feedback)

Individual *E*s informally pick *S*s they believe have high ESP abilities.

SELECTION STUDY
(No Feedback)

Screen groups of students and occasional individuals with 2 quick card guessing tests, score for each individual *S*.

—Invite to Confirmation Study if *S* scores above chance at .05 level+ *or* shows special promise

CONFIRMATION STUDY
(Feedback)

Each *S* individually tested with 2 runs on Aquarius, 2 on TCT, and 2 more on machine of choice.

—Invite to Training Study if *S* continues to score at .05 level+ *or* shows special promise

IMPLICIT
– CONTROL GROUP –

Thousands of *S*s in previous studies in which extinction/decline is well-nigh universal, regardless of experimental manipulations.

– EXPERIMENTAL GROUP –
TRAINING STUDY
(Feedback)

Each *S* individually tested for 20 runs on machine of his or her choice

Evaluate Results

FIG. 3. Overall procedure of the experiments

the others passed out response sheets to the students. The students had the option of not participating if they wished, but very few took this option. The students were told that this was a general test to see how much ESP we could find and, if they did very well on it, they might be contacted later for individual experimentation.

For the actual testing, the first run was designated a telepathy run, i.e., two experimenters acted as senders (agents) and looked at each card. A third experimenter, who could not see the cards and did not know their order, called a time signal approximately every five seconds, which was a cue for the senders to look at a new card; meanwhile, the students would have had a chance to put their responses down. This was too fast a pace for comfortable working, but it generally had to be adhered to because of the time limitations.

The second run was a clairvoyance run, i.e., a card was removed (face down) from the pack every five seconds, but it was not looked at. The score sheets were then collected, and the students departed for their next class. Within a few days a score sheet giving each student's number correct was posted in the classroom so that the students could have some feedback on how they had done.

Although the rushed conditions were far from psychologically optimal for eliciting ESP, we went to great pains to avoid giving any sensory cues, so that any high scores would have to be attributed to ESP and/or to purely statistical fluctuations.

Results. Our primary purpose in carrying out the Selection Study was to find high-scoring subjects, and the question of whether the population we sampled showed ESP as a group was of minor interest. Thus we were not compulsively careful in handling and storing the data sheets. Coupled with a six-month delay in analyzing the data of the studies, this resulted in the loss of a small but unknown number of data sheets. Further, this was not a random but a systematic loss of data sheets of high-scoring subjects, for individual experimenters would pull out these sheets in order to contact the subjects for participation in the Confirmation Study. We know that some of these data sheets were lost because subjects would appear later in the study sequence without any data sheets for the Selection Study, even though individual experimenters would recall picking those subjects because of high Selection Study scores. Thus an analysis of the overall results of the Selection Study would systematically underestimate the level of ESP in the University of California, Davis, student population.

Because of these considerations, we did not carry out a formal analysis of overall Selection Study results. In general, we tested over 1,500 subjects, and it was our impression that many more subjects than would be expected by chance met the individual criteria discussed below for going on to the Confirmation Study.

The formal criterion for being selected for the Confirmation Study was that a subject had to score at least at the .05 level of significance on one run, or on his total score on the two runs of the Selection Study. In practice this meant a score of nine or greater on either run, or a score of 15 or greater for the two runs combined. However, if an individual experimenter chose to believe that a subject had ESP ability even if it didn't show up in the Selection Study, he could run that subject through the Confirmation Study. A common criterion applied by experimenters was the presence of several hits in a row, or displacement on to the previous or following target, even if the total score did not meet the formal criterion.

Of the 70 subjects who participated in the Confirmation Study, 23 did not participate in the Selection Study at all, but began with the Confirmation Study procedure because individual experimenters had various reasons for believing that these subjects had ESP ability. Of the 47 subjects who did participate, 24 scored at the .01 level of significance or better, 6 at the .05 level, and 17 had non-significant formal scores. There were other significant-scoring subjects in the Selection Study who, for one reason or another, did not choose to participate in the Confirmation Study, so the preceding figures should not be used to estimate the overall results of the Selection Study.

In general, the Selection Study was quite successful in terms of finding a large number of subjects who met our criterion of showing significant ESP. Considering how rushed the study was, the results were excellent.

Confirmation Study

The purpose of the Confirmation Study was to eliminate from further training those few subjects who had met the .05 significance level criterion of the Selection Study by chance alone (or had gone on to the

Confirmation Study because of informal signs of promise, such as many displacements); the likelihood that any particular subject would meet that criterion in the Selection Study *and* score significantly in the Confirmation Study by chance alone is very small. It also served to adapt the subjects to the laboratory setting in which they would be working in the Training Study, as well as giving us a more adequate sample of each subject's ESP ability. We shall use this more adequate sample in later analyses as a rough measure of a subject's initial talent level before beginning the Training Study.

The Confirmation Study was the first introduction of the subjects to the two training instruments, so these instruments will now be described.

The Aquarius Model 100.   The Aquarius Model 100 ESP Trainer is a commercial instrument manufactured by the Aquarius Electronics Company of Albion, California, which is based on a machine built earlier by Russell Targ and David Hurt (Targ & Hurt, 1972). It is an attractive machine, built in a hardwood case. There are four non-illuminated slides with a non-illuminated push button by each, plus another push button in the center of these buttons labeled Pass. Figure 4 shows the panel arrangement. We modified the target slides provided by the manufacturer to ones we believed more obviously discriminable, viz., a cross on a blue background, square on yellow, star on red, and circle on green.

At any given time, the subject knows that the machine has randomly selected one of the four slides as the target, even though it is not lit. The subject's task is to push the button corresponding to the slide he thinks has already been selected.

The randomization is done entirely by the machine, by what is known as an "electronic roulette wheel" circuit. A block diagram of the entire machine circuit is shown in figure 5. The electronic roulette wheel consists of an oscillator oscillating at approximately one million Hertz (cycles/second), or one megahertz. Its output drives a counter which counts from one to four and repeats; so in a single second each output is selected about two hundred and fifty thousand times. The cycling of the counter, 1-2-3-4-1-2-3----3-4-1-2-etc., is like the spinning of a roulette wheel. The length of time a subject holds down his response button on the previous trial

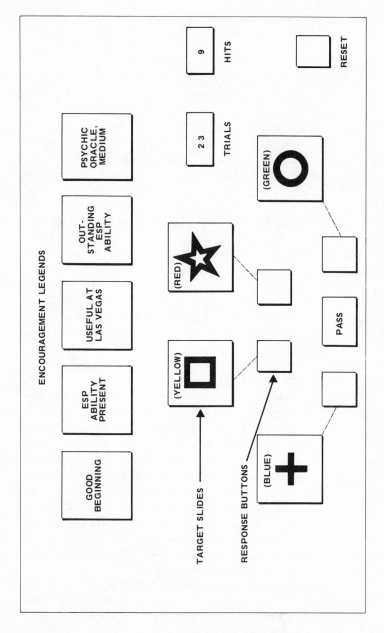

Fig. 4. Panel layout of the Aquarius Model 100 ESP Trainer

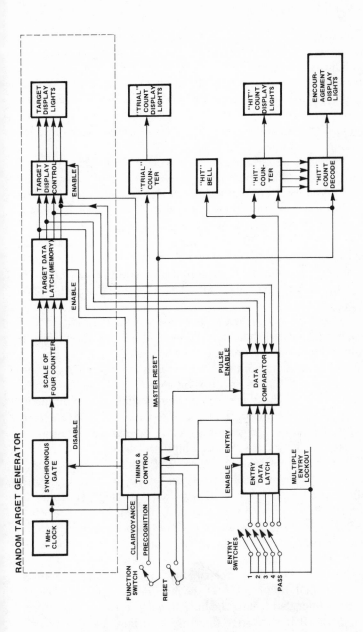

Fig. 5. Block diagram of the Aquarius Model 100 ESP Trainer. Reproduced by permission of Aquarius Electronics Company

determines the length of time that the oscillator is connected to the counting circuit, and thus the ultimate outcome of the selection. Since human response time is about four orders of magnitude greater than the speed at which the oscillator oscillates, as well as being subject to random factors which are also several orders of magnitude greater than the period at which the oscillator cycles, this results in a totally random selection, with an equal probability for each of the four targets.

The machines are checked for randomicity before being shipped from the factory. The factory test procedure is that each of the four targets must appear approximately equally in a run of 700 trials, i.e., each target does not show a statistically significant deviation from appearing one-fourth of the time. The machine is also tested by the runs tests (Siegel, 1956) to be sure that there are no sequential effects, i.e., that each target selection is totally independent of the previous target selection.[2] Our tests of the Aquarius shortly after the end of the Training Study showed it to be still satisfactorily random.[3]

As soon as a subject pushed his response button, the slide (and its corresponding button) that the machine had selected lit up, giving the subject immediate feedback as to whether he had been right or wrong and what the target had been. In addition, if the subject had selected the right button, a pleasant-sounding chime inside the machine sounded. This was the immediate feedback and reinforcement to the subjects, important in the application of learning theory. In addition, the Aquarius machine has encouragement lights: after 6 hits a transparency lights up, saying "Good Beginning"; after 8 hits one lights up saying "ESP Ability Present" (this is not actually at a statistically significant level); at 10 hits it says "Useful at Las Vegas"; at 12 hits it says "Outstanding ESP Ability"; and at 14 hits its says "Psychic Oracle, Medium." Both experimenters and subjects generally felt these encouragement legends were a little silly, but they were a useful relative indicator of performance in a single run.

The machine is designed for runs of 25 trials. A trial counter keeps count of all trials, and locks the machine at 25 trials. There is also a hit counter that counts the hits. In our procedure, the subject pressed a signal button after finishing his trials, and the experimenter returned to the room to read the hit total from the counter.

Our experiment was procedurally a telepathy experiment, although technically we would say it was a GESP experiment since we did not know if the subjects got their ESP information from the senders' minds or the state of the machine itself. To make this a telepathy experiment, a special indicator panel showing which target had been selected was looked at by the experimenter, acting as sender (agent). It also showed which response button the subject pushed. Figure 6 shows the room arrangements used. The subject was in a room by himself with the Aquarius (there was no way he could readily tamper with it), and the experimenter-sender watched the telepathy adapter panel in a room approximately 70 feet away. Two heavy closed doors and 69 feet of carpeted corridor separated the sender and the subject, and, since the sender kept quiet while attempting to concentrate, there were no sensory cues for the subject to respond to.

Ten-Choice Trainer Machine. Figure 7 shows the subject's console of the ten-choice training instrument (TCT, Ten-Choice Trainer). This console, about two feet across, was in a horizontal position in front of the seated subject. On any given trial, he was faced with a circle of 10 unlit pilot lamps, plus a Pass button. When the signal lamp in the center of the circle, the Ready Light, came on, he knew that his experimenter-sender, in a different room had selected one of the ten unlit pilot lamps as a target and was trying to send it. A playing card from ace to 10 was beside each unlit pilot lamp, so the number of the playing card was an additional identifier of the selected target. After the Ready Light came on, the subject had to decide which light he thought had been selected as target and push the button beside it. As with the Aquarius machine, the correct target then immediately lit and, if the subject had chosen the correct target, a pleasant chime sounded inside the console. Thus again the subject received immediate and complete feedback on the correctness or incorrectness of his choice.

The experimenter's TCT console was basically the same as the subject's: there was an identical-size circle of 10 pilot lights and a switch beside each to operate for the card chosen as a target. The console and associated equipment are shown in figure 8. This

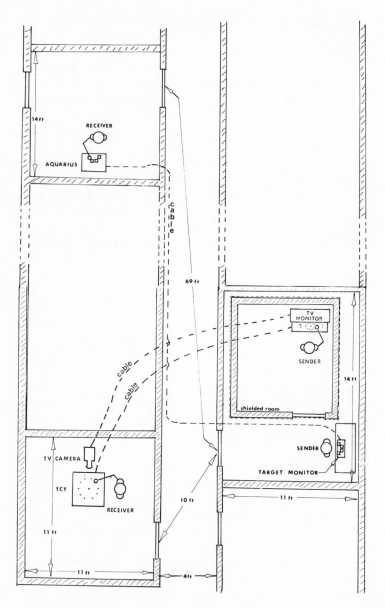

FIG. 6. Layout of the experimental laboratories

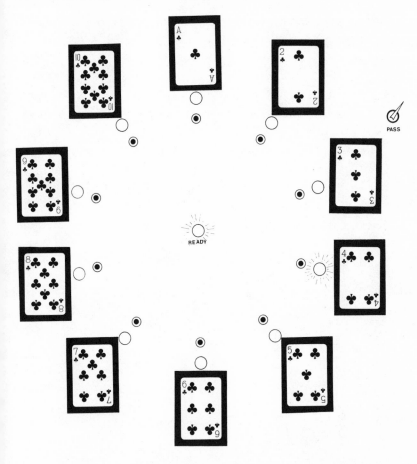

Fɪɢ. 7.   Subject's console, Ten-Choice Trainer. Target No. 4 is shown as lit after subject has made his response.

console also contained trials and hits counters. As with the Aquarius machine, the experimenter-sender got immediate feedback as to what target the subject had chosen, and its correctness or incorrectness. If the response was correct, an additional red lamp also lit on the experimenter's console. Technical details of the TCT are presented in appendix 1. The TCT was also used in runs of 25.

In order to generate the target sequence for each run, a commonly

Fig. 8.   Experimenter-sender's console, Ten-Choice Trainer.
Target No. 2 has been selected.

used card randomization procedure, known as an open deck, was used until an electronic random number generator was built to replace it. The experimenter had a large flat box beside him in which the ace to 10 cards from 10 identical-backed decks were placed, face down. This total deck of 400 cards, containing 40 aces, 40 twos, etc., was roughly shuffled with both hands by sliding the cards (always face down) about, under, and over each other for a minute or two. The experimenter then blindly pulled a batch of from 30 to 40 face-down cards from this large pool. Although there were only 25 trials in a run, the extra cards were in case the subject used the Pass option.

This blindly selected subdeck was then dovetail shuffled by hand several times, without the experimenter looking at the cards, to further randomize the order. The subdeck was then put face down beside the experimenter's TCT console, and he would turn over the top card, regularly down through the deck, for the target on each successive trial.

This rather elaborate procedure is necessary because you cannot give immediate feedback on target cards from an ordinary closed deck; if a subject keeps track of what has already come up, he can alter his guessing strategy to aim at target cards that have not yet been played, thus artifactually raising his scores. In a 40-card, ace-to-10 deck, e.g., the subject may remember that 3 aces had already appeared, which would mean that the probability of any remaining card being an ace was only one-fourth of what it had been, so not guessing an ace would be excellent strategy. In our subdeck drawn from 10 decks, however, if 3 aces have already appeared there is not just 1 ace potentially left in the deck but 37 of them, so the probability of the next card being an ace is only trivially lowered from one-tenth.

The open deck card randomization procedure was used for target generation in the Confirmation Study. An electronic random number generator, of similar design to that used in the Aquarius, was used for target generation on the TCT throughout the Training Study.

The electronic randomizer differed from that used in the Aquarius machine in that our oscillator ran at 5 rather than 1 megahertz. Figure 9 gives the circuit of our randomizer, designed and constructed by

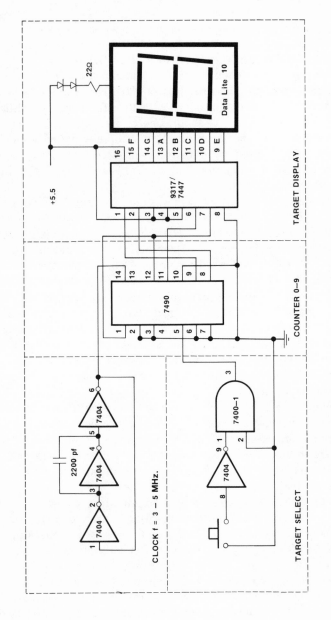

Fig. 9. Circuit of the random number generator used with the Ten-Choice Trainer. Integrated circuits are Signetics types 7404, 7400, 7447, and 7490, and the seven-segment display is a Litronix Data Lite 10.

D.J. Redington. The output of the randomizer is displayed as a numeral from zero (for card 10) to nine on a readout device, so the experimenter would push the button on the randomizer after each response by the subject, read the newly selected target, and throw the appropriate switch on the TCT.[4] Chi-square tests for equal frequency of selection and independence of pairs of sequencing effects on 1,000 trial blocks, taken before the introduction of this randomizer into the experiments and after their end, showed no significant departures from randomicity.

Differences between Instruments. The TCT and its use differed from the Aquarius machine in a variety of ways. First was the one-tenth probability of any particular target being the one selected, rather than the one-fourth probability. This means that only two or three hits (2.5 on the average) would be expected by chance in a run of 25, so the subject would have fewer hits and more misses. To put it positively, he would less frequently be falsely reinforced through having hit by chance. There were no encouragement lights on the TCT subject's console, and the hit and trial counters were not visible to the subject, only to the experimenter-sender. There were charts of P values of various scoring levels posted by each machine, though, so subjects knew when they were doing well.

The arrangement of the rooms for the TCT training is shown in figure 6. The experimenter-sender sat inside a semishielded Faraday cage. This was a sound attenuating room, constructed of plywood walls over a standard 2 by 4 frame, with fiberglass insulation between the walls, acoustic tile lining the inside walls and ceiling, and a rug on the floor. A ventilating fan made a soft hum inside the room. The room was totally covered with thin copper sheeting, and its door was closed, but we call this *semi*shielded because the necessary connecting cables between the subject's and the experimenter-sender's console, running through a small hole in the wall, meant that the shielding lost some of its integrity, electromagnetically speaking. The electrically shielded aspect of this room may be significant for, even though the shielding was imperfect, Puharich (1973) and Vasiliev (1963) reported that shielding increases ESP scoring. This inner room also rested on rubber tires to shock-mount it from building vibration. The experimenter-sender was thus isolated from the subject by three closed doors, partial electromagnetic shielding, and a distance of about 20 feet.

Because of the circular arrangement of the target lights on the TCT, many subjects would slowly scan their hand around the periphery of the circle looking for "hot" and "cold" sensations or the like in trying to make their choice.[5] To give the experimenter-sender more feedback on this aspect of the subject's behavior, all through the Confirmation and Training studies a closed-circuit TV camera (video only) was suspended above the subject's console, transmitting to a screen above the experimenter's console, so that the experimenter could watch the subject's hand motions and see whether he was getting closer to or further from the target, when he hesitated, etc. This was the kind of feedback to the sender that, I argued (chapter 1), probably made the old Brugman (1922) experiment so successful. To help the experimenter to keep the correct target in mind, we put over the TV screen a transparent template that incorporated a small light-emitting diode over the TV image of each target. When the experimenter actually threw the switch to select a target, the light-emitting diode on the screen showed a red glow over the appropriate target, enabling him to concentrate fully on the TV screen. The experimenters reported that when a subject used this circular scanning, they got very involved in trying to send "hotter" and "colder," "push now," "go back," etc., kinds of thoughts, as well as or instead of the number of the target.

Note that for the Aquarius machine the speed of response was controlled by the subject: he could press the buttons on the machine as rapidly as he desired. This could be very frustrating for the experimenters, as they could make no real attempt to send under rapid response conditions.[6] On the TCT, the speed of response was controlled by the experimenter: there was always a lapse of several seconds between the subject's indicating his response and the Ready Light for the next trial coming on, as the experimenter needed time to write down the subject's previous response, select the next target (either from the open deck or the randomizer), and then manually throw the appropriate control switch.

Experimenter-Subject Interaction. We attempted to create a re-laxed, comfortable, informal atmosphere for both the Confirmation Study and the Training Study. Thus the subjects' rooms were made quite comfortable; they were decorated with Indian print bed-spreads and were pleasant by the standards of contemporary youth. Subjects were shown the whole experimental setup the first time they came to the laboratory, and all procedures were explained fully to them. We tried always to take an attitude of being totally open and friendly with the subjects. Early in the course we had discussed the covert hostilities that subjects can build up in the traditional, "colonial" paradigm of psychological experimentation, drawing on the experimenters' own experiences as subjects in other psychology experiments to make this personally real.

For the Confirmation Study, each subject was given a total of six runs of 25 trials each, with the same experimenter as sender all the way through. Two runs were on the TCT and two were on the Aquarius; which came first was decided by the vagaries of when the rooms were available to fit the schedules of a particular experi-menter and subject. Then the subject had two more runs on whichever machine he chose.[7] At the end of each run of 25, the experimenter would go back to the subject's room, talk to him and encourage him, and generally keep up a positive relationship.

At the end of the Confirmation Study, each subject was thanked and told that he might be contacted further for more extensive work. Subjects almost universally found the procedure quite in-teresting and were glad to participate. No subjects received any monetary rewards for participation in the Confirmation or Training Studies; a few received a small amount of credit for experimental participation in elementary psychology courses they were taking.

Results of the Confirmation Study. Table 2 presents the overall results of the Confirmation Study. Recall that by chance alone we expect mean run scores of 6.25 for the Aquarius and 2.50 for the TCT.

Seventy subjects were tested on the Aquarius machine and 68 on the TCT. Overall, there were 1,501 hits on the Aquarius when only

TABLE 2   **Confirmation Study Results**

AQUARIUS			TCT		
Subjects[a]	Hits/ Expected	Mean/ Run	Subjects[a]	Hits/ Expected	Mean/ Run
70	1,501/1,437.5	6.53 P = .03 (1-tailed)	68	635/477.5	3.32 P = 1x10⁻¹⁴ (1-tailed)

[a]While all subjects were supposed to be tested on both the Aquarius and the TCT, occasionally subjects did not complete testing on both, so the number of subjects in the Aquarius and TCT analyses differs.

1,437.5 were expected by chance, a deviation of 63.5 hits over chance. This would occur by chance approximately 3 in 100 times, so GESP was being demonstrated on the Aquarius machine. For the TCT, there were 635 hits when 477.5 would be expected by chance, a deviation of 157.5 above chance. This has a probability of 10^{-14}. These are exceptionally significant results, which show ESP operating with the TCT. Thus a pattern emerges which continued in the rest of the studies, viz., that results on the TCT were generally more significant than on the Aquarius.

Learning in the Confirmation Study. The Confirmation Study procedurally constituted a short training period, since immediate feedback was given, so we can ask the question whether there was any evidence of learning in it. Learning theory would not make a clear prediction for so brief a period, given the contrary effects of adaptation, but it is interesting to look at empirically. To examine this, we looked at whichever machine the subject had done four runs on and compared scores on the first pair of runs with those on the second pair of runs. This meant ignoring such niceties as whether or not the two runs on the other machine had come in between or later. For a few cases where a subject had actually done five runs instead of four (in spite of the instructions), we simply skipped the middle score. If there were six or more runs, the subject was not used in this analysis. These omissions make the totals in table 3 less than those given in table 2.

Table 3 shows the total number of hits in the first and second halves of the Confirmation Study for all subjects; the figures are then broken down for the subjects going on to complete the Training Study and those not doing so. For the Aquarius machine, by inspection, the total number of hits in the first and second halves is essentially the same. For the TCT, there is a suggestion ($P < .10$) of a decline in performance from the first to the second half of the Confirmation Study. This is not so, by inspection, for subjects going on to complete the Training Study, but subjects not completing the Training Study dropped from 122 hits in the first half to 95 in the second half. A t test for correlated populations shows that this is almost a significant drop in mean score ($t = 1.78$, $df = 16$, $P < .10$, 2-tailed).

TABLE 3   **Total Hits in the Confirmation Study**

	AQUARIUS		TCT	
	First Half	Second Half	First Half	Second Half
All subjects	543	554	191	159[a]
Subjects completing Training Study	195	205	69	64
Subjects not completing Training Study	348	349	122	95[a]

[a]P difference $< .10$ (2-tailed).

An alternative explanation of this apparent decline, however, occurs when we recall that the subjects had the option of choosing which machine to do the last two of their six trials on. If by chance alone they had scored high on one machine and not on the other, it would be only natural to choose to complete the study on the one they had scored high on. Regression to the mean, a return to chance scoring from what was only a meaningless fluctuation in the first place, would artifactually introduce a decline which had nothing to do with learning or extinction of ESP ability.

To check this possibility, we looked at deviation of scores from chance expectancy for runs one through six, ignoring which machine was used. The picture that then emerges suggests learning, not extinction. The mean deviation from chance for the six runs, in order, was -.688, -.838, +.950, +1.100, -.184, and +.875, which has a positive slope of +.28, although this does not reach statistical significance for such a small N. These subjects started off about half a correct ESP response below chance and came up to half a correct response above chance. For the time being it would be best to conclude that performance in the Confirmation Study was relatively steady.

Did the Selection Study Predict Later Performance?

How well did Selection Study scores predict performance in the Confirmation Study? Would a really good scorer in one study remain a good scorer in the next? To answer this question we must look at the correlation between subjects' scores in the two studies. Note, however, that because of the nature of the selection process, namely, by usually taking only people from the Selection Study who were exceptionally high scorers, we reduced the range of variation and so automatically reduced the correlation coefficients, possibly obliterating significant relationships. Results are shown in table 4, with Spearman correlation coefficients between mean scores of subjects in each study.

It is of interest to note that subjects who went on to complete the Training Study generally showed strong scoring differences between the two machines they worked on in the Confirmation Study. There is a highly significant negative correlation (r = -.69, P < .0005, 2-tailed) between the mean score on one machine and that on the other, although some subjects did well on both. For subjects who did not go on to complete the Training Study, the correlation was also negative (r = -.25), but insignificant.

Training Study

In order to qualify for inclusion in the Training Study, the formal rule was that a subject must have scored at least at the .05 level of significance on a single run (a rough measure of "peak" potential) on either machine in the Confirmation Study, or on the total score for a single machine. As in selecting for the Confirmation Study, an individual experimenter could continue a subject who did not meet this formal criterion if he thought he had very good reason to do so.

TABLE 4   **Correlations in Selection and Confirmation Studies**

	Aquarius Performances	TCT Performances
Subjects completing Training Study	–.13 (N = 12)	.30 (N = 11)
Subjects not completing Training Study	.26 (N = 33)	.30[a] (N = 32)
All subjects	.03 (N = 45)	.22 (N = 43)

[a]P < .05 (1-tailed).

Forty-two subjects had at least 1 run in the Training Study. Seven of these had only 1 run each here, and apparently had not been through the Confirmation Study (no data sheets), while 10 subjects had 2 to 14 runs on one or the other machine, sometimes dividing their runs between the machines. For the sake of accounting for all data, these improperly run subjects and incomplete results will be analyzed in an overall look, but, in accordance with an a priori decision, only the subjects who completed all 20 runs in the Training Study will be considered in detail.[8]

Because this was an a priori decision on our part, we could not optionally stop at some point in data analysis where chance trends favored our hypotheses. The question of subjects stopping participation at some point of their own choosing is more complex however. Since the primary analysis for learning effects must be made on an individual subject basis, analyzing results of subjects who completed the Training Study will not be affected by subjects who dropped out. For our analysis of the relation of overall slope of the learning curve and level of ESP ability across subjects, however, a falsely positive correlation could be generated if subjects who were declining dropped out while those who weren't completed the study, so we shall look at the data of incomplete subjects where relevant.

The experimental procedure in the Training Study was basically the same as that in the Confirmation Study, except that each subject worked with only one machine of his choice for all 20 runs. Again, each subject had his individual experimenter, and the experimenters felt they were successful in maintaining a friendly, informal relationship with their subjects throughout the experiment.[9] Gaines Thomas' (El) account of his relationships with his subjects, presented in chapter 5, further specifies the kind of experimenter-subject relationships we had.

Note, however, that while the experimental procedure was basically the same as in the Confirmation Study, the psychological conditions of this study were significantly different. In the beginning of the Training Study, subjects were informed that this was the important study, that the others had been only preliminaries. They (the subjects) were *special*, and were expected not only to remain special, but we hoped that, by learning to use their ESP better, they would become even more special. Thus, in spite of our efforts to keep things relaxed, the Training Study subjects were under a certain amount of pressure. Alterations in psychological conditions in ESP experiments have frequently been observed to change performance levels.

Sessions in the Training Study usually occurred irregularly, owing to the vagaries arising from many experimenters needing to schedule the same room. Intervals between sessions ranged from a day to several weeks. The number of runs within a single session ranged from 1 to 13, depending on how fast a subject worked, which machine he was using, and whether the laboratory was available for only an hour (typical) or several hours.

While the learning theory application has been presented primarily in terms of allowing the receiver, the subject, to learn to use his or her ESP abilities better, it is important to note that in both the Confirmation and Training Studies we gave complete feedback to the experimenter, who was trying to act as a sender, as well as to the receiver. Thus our experimental setup allows for learning by the sender/receiver team as a system, as well as for either of them learning alone.

Overall Results of the Training Study. The learning theory application, as formulated to date, does not deal with ESP-missing, although the general parapsychological literature and the results of the pilot study indicate that it will eventually have to be taken into account. Evaluating ESP-missing means using two-tailed statistical tests to examine extreme deviations both above and below chance, so we shall use these tests in evaluating the results of the Training Study except where specific, a priori predictions were made.[10]

Table 5 presents the results of the Training Study for all subjects run, with a breakdown into subjects who actually completed the Training Study and those who did not. For all subjects, results were highly significant. On the Aquarius machine, there were 2,405 hits, a deviation of 161.25 above chance ($P = 4 \times 10^{-5}$). For the TCT, there were 828 hits, a deviation of 233 above chance ($P = 1 \times 10^{-23}$).

Breaking these figures down, the subjects not completing the Training Study showed insignificant results on both the Aquarius machine and the TCT.[11] Subjects completing the training, however, showed exceptionally significant results. For the Aquarius machine, there were 2,006 hits, 137.25 more than chance ($P = 4 \times 10^{-4}$). For the TCT, there were 722 hits, where only 500 would be expected by chance ($P = 2 \times 10^{-25}$).

Now let us consider the results in detail for subjects who completed the Training Study.

TABLE 5 **Training Study, Overall Results**

	AQUARIUS			
	Subjects	Hits/ Expected	Mean/ Run	P (2-tailed)
All subjects starting study	21	2,405/2,243.75	6.70	4×10^{-5}
Subjects completing study	15	2,006/1,868.75	6.71	4×10^{-4}
Subjects dropping out early	6	399/375	6.65	ns
	TCT			
	Subjects	Hits/ Expected	Mean/ Run	P (2-tailed)
All subjects starting study	21	828/595	3.48	1×10^{-23}
Subjects completing study	10	722/500	3.61	2×10^{-25}
Subjects dropping out early	11	106/95	2.79	ns

Aquarius—Presence of ESP. Fifteen subjects (six men, nine women) completed the training on the Aquarius machine. Eight of these had qualified for the Training Study at the .01 or better level of significance in the Confirmation Study, four at the .05 level, and one at the .10 level. For two of the subjects the Confirmation Study data sheets had been lost. Table 6 presents the results by individual subject for the Aquarius machine, arranged in order of decreasing scores.

TABLE 6   **Training Study, Aquarius Results**

Subject	Hits/ Expected	Mean/ Run	P (2-tailed)	Overall Slope	Mean Within- Session Slope
E7S24	162/125	8.10	1×10^{-4}	.22[a]	.19
E2S9	155/125	7.75	2×10^{-3}	-.07	-.27
E7S22	151/125	7.55	.008	-.09	.41
E4S12	146/119	7.68	004	-.01	-.80
E8S25	147/125	7.35	.02	-.08	.32
E1S6	141/125	7.05	.10	.01	-.20
E7S23	139/125	6.95	ns	.07	.20
E10S31	133/125	6.65	ns	.03	-.66
E6S1	133/125	6.65	ns	.09	....[c]
E4S13[b]	132/125	6.60	ns	-.17	-.13
E5S15	124/125	6.20	ns	.02	.40
E8S26	122/125	6.10	ns	-.06	-.62
E6S21	116/125	5.80	ns	-.08	....[c]
E9S29[b]	104/125	5.20	.04	-.17	-1.93
E6S20	101/125	5.05	.01	.02	....[c]
Total of 15 subjects	2,006/1,869	6.72	4×10^{-4}	-.01	-.47

[a] P = .01 (1-tailed).

[b] Variance greater than expected, P < .05 (1-tailed).

[c] E6 copied his data in a way that did not allow computation of within-session slopes.

Five of the 15 subjects showed results that were individually significant at the .05 level or better for scoring above chance. Another subject, S13, while not scoring significantly above chance, showed so much variability that his results also probably reflect the operation of ESP. Two other subjects scored significantly *below* chance, one at the .04 level (with significant variability), the other at the .01 level, suggesting psi-missing. The best subject made 162 hits where she would be expected by chance to score 125 ($P = 1 \times 10^{-4}$). Individuals' runs varied from a low of zero hits in a run of 25 ($P = .007$, 1-tailed) to a high of 13 ($P < .002$, 1-tailed). The group as a whole had a mean of 6.72 hits per run versus a chance expectancy of 6.25 hits, which can be roughly interpreted as meaning that a genuine ESP response occurred at least once every other run, on the average. I stress *at least*, as this mean is lowered by the scores of the two subjects who scored significantly below chance.

Although there is a goodly amount of ESP in these Training Study results, with 5 of the 15 subjects showing individually significant psi-hitting, it is interesting to ask why 10 of them did *not* show individually significant psi-hitting, given that the two-step selection procedure used made it very unlikely that a subject with no ESP ability would have made it into the Training Study. That is, using the .05 level of significance for individual subjects as a criterion for going from one study to the next, we would average five false positives, subjects mistakenly going on, for every hundred subjects tested. The combined probability of a subject scoring at least at the .05 level in two sequential tests, however, is $.05 \times .05 = .0025$ or less; so, having started by screening 1,500+ subjects we would expect only four or five at the most to end up in the Training Study in spite of having no real ESP ablility. Additionally, two other lines of explanation may be proposed.

First, 4 of the 10 subjects do not have Selection Study data available; either it was lost or they went directly into the Confirmation Study because their experimenter believed they had ESP for other reasons. The possibility of picking subjects with no ESP or poorly controlled ESP is, of course, higher for a one-stage selection process than for a two-stage one.

Second, the increased psychological pressure inherent in participating in the Training Study may have inhibited or distorted some subjects' ESP abilities. S13, for example, continued to show ESP in terms of significant variability in scoring, but could not focus it for hitting, Two of the other 10 subjects. S29 and S20, switched to a significant psi-missing pattern. Since we did not collect target and call data for every response from the Aquarius subjects, we can only speculate that distortion of the ESP process may have occurred for some of these other subjects, but it is a possibility to be checked in future studies.

Aquarius—Learning. Table 6 also shows two measures of learning for each subject, the overall slope of the regression line fitted to all runs in the Training Study, and the average within-session slope. The number of sessions varied from two to five per subject, with 2 to 13 runs within each session.

For the group as a whole, the mean overall slope is essentially zero. Looking at the overall slopes of individual subjects, most were essentially zero, none was significantly negative, and one was significantly positive (for S24)[12]—a slope of $+.22$, which indicates an average gain of one ESP hit about every five runs (125 trials). S24's performance is shown in figure 10, along with the fitted regression line. These results support the learning theory application in that the usual decline effect (extinction) found in almost all ESP repeated-guessing studies is absent, and one subject showed a significantly positive slope.

S24 was an enthusiastic subject, who came into the experiment with the attitude that "I know I have ESP, and I'm going to show you!" She worked at a slow to moderate rate, and ran her fingers over the response buttons to get a "feel" for the correct one.

When performance is inspected by *sessions* (a temporal and psychological unit), it becomes clear that a subject's overall slope can sometimes be a very misleading descriptor. Thus, slope was also computed for each session, and the average of these within-session slopes is also presented in table 6. These mean within-session slopes do not, to my knowledge, lend themselves to any clear test of statistical significance, so they must be regarded primarily as descriptors here.[13] As descriptors, they reveal that there is probably more learning of ESP in the data than can be picked out by formal analysis. For example, consider the performance of S22, shown in figure 11. He had three sessions, with slopes, respectively, of $+.13$, -40, and $+1.5$, for an average within-session slope of $+.41$, quite

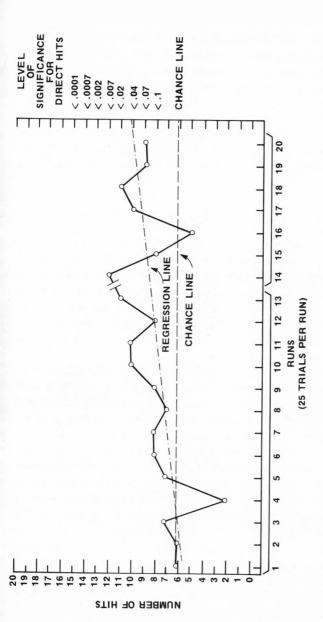

Fig. 10. Performance of S24, computer plot

different from his overall slope of -.09. The discrepancy arises partly from an insignificant, overall decline in ESP performance, but primarily from drops *between* sessions. That is, this subject showed a pattern that others also showed, of what looked like learning (positive slope) within some sessions, but a loss of whatever ability he'd learned between sessions.

Although the formal data analyses for the Aquarius support the learning theory application, then, inspection of some of the individual performance curves in ways not readily susceptible to formal analysis suggests even more support.

Aquarius—ESP Ability and Slope. One of the predictions in applying learning theory to learning ESP ability was the need for a fair amount of ESP ability to begin with in order for the effects of feedback and learning to overcome the inherent confusion induced by reinforcement of chance correct responses, boredom, loss of motivation, etc. Ignoring the problems created by the possible non-linearity of this prediction and the problem created by motivated psi-missing, this prediction takes the rough form of positive correlation between overall ESP ability (measured by scoring level above chance) and overall slope.

In the Training Study, there is a correlation of +.35 between mean ESP score and slope for the Aquarius subjects, although this is not statistically significant.[14] Overall slopes in the Training Study were also correlated with ESP scoring level on the Aquarius in the earlier Confirmation Study for subjects for whom these data were available (13 subjects), but this correlation was not significant ($r = +.29$). Performance on the TCT in the Confirmation Study was almost significantly related ($r = +.44$, $P < .10$) to overall slope in the Training Study, however, even though most of the subjects completing the Training Study on the Aquarius trainer had only two runs on the TCT in the Confirmation Study.

Aquarius—Training Study vs. Selection and Confirmation Studies. Since we used performance in earlier studies as a criterion for admission to later studies for most subjects, how well did earlier performance predict Training Study performance?

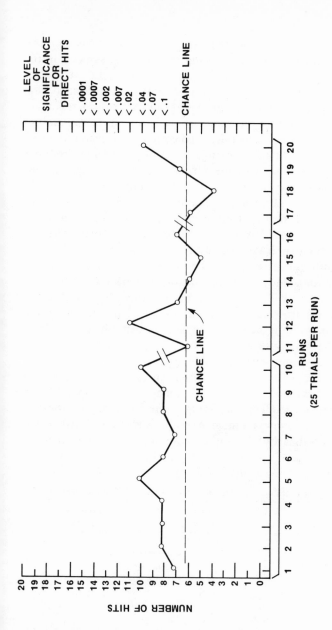

FIG. 11. Performance of S22, computer plot

This is not as easy a question to answer as it seems, for two reasons. First, the actual ESP testing of individual subjects in the Selection and Confirmation Studies was very brief and therefore not too reliable a measure of their actual ESP ability. Second, the procedure of selecting only high-scoring subjects to progress from study to study reduces the range of variation of scores and so mathematically reduces any calculated correlations, even if the true correlation is high. Since some subjects went on to later studies even though they did not meet the formal criterion of high scores, however, there are some low scores to widen our range.

Taking mean hits/run in the Training Study as our main ESP measure, we then find that mean hits/run in the Selection Study correlates with this +.47 (N = 7, non-significant), and mean hits/run in the Confirmation Study (Aquarius trainer) correlates +.27 (N = 13, non-significant). If we use the best run score on the Aquarius in the Confirmation Study as a rough measure of peak ESP ability, this correlates +.50 with Training Study performance (N = 13, P < .05, 1-tailed). Thus there is some predictability of performance: the better a subject did in the earlier studies, the better he was liable to do in the Training Study.

It has often been noted that the very first ESP attempts by a subject produce the best scores; there is an excitement and enthusiasm in the first few trials or runs that may not occur again. Since the Confirmation and Training Studies were essentially identical in procedure, we can compare them to see if this effect occurred. Table 7 shows this comparison for the 13 Aquarius subjects on whom all relevant data were collected, using performance data on the Aquarius from the Confirmation Study.

TABLE 7 **Scoring Rates on Aquarius in Confirmation and Training Studies**

	Confirmation Study	Training Study
Mean scores	7.41	6.75
	$P_{diff} < .10$ (2-tailed)	
Best run scores	9.76	10.53
	ns	

There was a peaking in performance in the Confirmation Study, with a suggestive drop in the Training Study to a sustained performance, on the average, for mean scores, with a non-significant suggestion that peak ESP potential (best run scores) might have gone up in the Training Study. While this might be interpreted as some immediate extinction of ESP ability despite the feedback, it is questionable because of the psychological distinction between the two studies, the long time gap between them, and the slight (but non-significant) increase in performance from the first to the second half of the Confirmation Study.

The drop in mean performance came entirely from those subjects who did not show individually significant hitting or who switched to psi-missing in the Training Study. The Aquarius subject who showed clear evidence of learning, S24, showed a small rise in performance.

TCT—Presence of ESP. Ten subjects (two men, eight women) completed 20 training runs each on the TCT, and their results are shown in table 8. In terms of being selected from the Confirmation Study, nine of them had scored at the .01 level of significance or better, and one at the .05 level.

The left-hand portion of table 8 shows the direct (ON) hits for each subject. As a group, the results are highly significant, with 722 hits when only 500 should have occurred by chance ($P = 2 \times 10^{-25}$). Five of the subjects showed individually significant results with probabilities of 4×10^{-5} or better for psi-hitting. One subject scored quite low, only 39 hits with 50 expected by chance, and this result is suggestive of psi-missing.

Individual significances went up as high as 124 hits when 50 were expected ($P = 4 \times 10^{-28}$). The results of this outstanding subject (S3) are shown in the lower curve of figure 12. She scored at significance levels of .05 or better for 17 of her 20 runs for ON hits. With a mean score of 6.2 hits/run instead of the expected 2.5, this is roughly three-and-a-half ESP responses in addition to guessing in each run. Details of the behavior and experience of this subject and the other four significantly scoring subjects on the TCT are given in chapter 5.

Scores on individual runs over all 10 subjects ranged from a low of

TABLE 8   Training Study, TCT Results

Subject	MAIN ESP RESULTS			LEARNING		DISPLACEMENT EFFECTS			
	ON Hits/ Expected	Mean/ Run	P (2-tailed)	Overall Slope	Mean Within-Session Slope	−1 Hits/ Expected	+1 Hits/ Expected	ON +(±1) Hits/ Expected	P (2-tailed)
E1S3	124/50	6.20	4×10^{-28}	.14	1.90	45/50	45/50	214/150	2×10^{-10}
E1S5	103/50	5.15	2×10^{-14}	−.03	−.00	44/50	57/50	204/150	2×10^{-7}
E1S4	81/50	4.05	4×10^{-6}	−.01	−.05	49/50	47/50	177/150	8×10^{-3}
E1S2	80/50	4.00	8×10^{-6}	−.02	−.01	66/50[a]	59/50	205/150	1×10^{-7}
E1S1	78/50	3.90	4×10^{-5}	.02	−.12	64/50[a]	44/50	186/150	4×10^{-4}
E13S17	59/50	2.95	ns	.02	.45	53/50	57/50	169/150	.06
E5S14	57/50	2.85	ns	−.10	−.36	49/50	51/50	157/150	ns
E2S7	54/50	2.70	ns	.03	−.16	61/50	46/50	161/150	ns
E11S32	47/50	2.35	ns	−.07	−.20	45/50	45/50	137/150	ns
E4S11	39/50	1.95	.10	−.05	−.20	60/50	53/50	152/150	ns
Total of 10 subjects	722/500	3.61	2×10^{-25}	−.01	.13	536/500[a]	504/500	1,762/1,500	1×10^{-15}

[a] P = .02 (2-tailed).

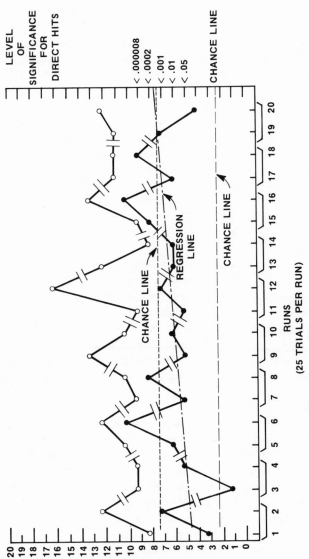

FIG. 12. Performance of S3, computer plot. Lower line is plot on direct hits, upper line on direct + near hits.

zero (which could readily occur by chance) to a high of 10 ($P \approx 10^{-11}$).

For the group of 10 subjects, there was a mean of 3.61 direct hits per run versus the 2.5 hits per run expected by chance, suggesting that there was one genuine ESP response on every run, on the average.

TCT—Spatial Focusing. A simple evaluation of the number of direct hits does not do justice to the TCT results. Because many subjects scanned the target circle by moving their hands around it, and because many subjects and experimenters conceived of the target in spatial position terms as well as or in preference to the numbers 1 through 10, it is legitimate to look at responses which were not direct (ON) hits but which were "Near" hits, immediately counterclockwise (-1) or clockwise (+1) spatial displacements to the correct target.

In order to collect data on possible spatial displacement, each experimenter filled out a prepared score sheet of what the target was and what the subject's response was for each trial, as well as when the Pass option was used. The number of hits from this hand record was checked against the number on the hit counter at the end of each run. This eliminates the possibility of systematic recording errors for ON hits, but there may be some slight errors in the spatial displacement data, so the following analyses are suggestive rather than absolutely firm.

The sixth and seventh columns in table 8 present the -1 and +1 displacement scores. The -1 hits occurred significantly more often than chance expectancy. Two of the 10 subjects were individually significant at the .05 level or better on -1 hits. They (S1 and S2) were subjects whose direct hits were significantly greater than chance, suggesting that in addition to their well-focused ESP abilities they also had some poorly focused ESP ability which displaced counterclockwise. A third subject (S7) scored suggestively high on counterclockwise displacement, although not on direct hits, suggesting that all of her ESP ability was improperly focused.

The final two columns of table 8 show results if we consider the selected target plus both the -1 and the +1 displacement targets as the actual ESP target, a "larger" target with a probability of .3 of being called on each trial, rather than .1. All five subjects who were individually significant on direct hits remain significant here, although with some change in rank order. A sixth subject (S17) almost reaches individual significance on this larger target, and the subject whose performance suggested psi-missing on direct hits (S11) now shows chance results.

Visual inspection of performance curves on individual subjects for ON plus Near hits indicates that the curves rise and fall in close parallelism most of the time (see figure 12), but there are occasional striking exceptions where, for example, the ON plus Near hits rise dramatically. This suggests that the ESP is still functioning but is not as clearly "focused" on the designated target, so close attention should be paid to Near hits in future studies.

Although we made no predictions about possible spatial displacement of ESP other than the +1 and -1 Near hits, we did examine possible hits on the other possible displacements for the 10 subjects, viz., -4, -3, -2, +2, +3, +4, and (±)5. All of these showed deviations below chance, particularly the -4 displacement (428 hits when 500 were expected by chance), as responses were drawn off from them to produce the 722 ON hits.

Since we have trial by trial data for the TCT subjects, we can take a more detailed look at the question of why 5 of these 10 highly selected subjects did not continue to show individually significant hitting in the Training Study. Two of them (S7 and S32) began directly with the Confirmation Study, so there was only a one-step selection process involved, not a two-step one. The possibility that they scored high originally through chance fluctuation rather than ESP, while still quite unlikely, is more likely than for those subjects who went through the two-step selection process. The possibility of insufficient selection is more unlikely for S7, however, as she showed suggestive displacement hitting on the -1 target.

Of the other three subjects who went through the two-step selection procedure but did not continue to score above chance in an individually significant manner, one (S11) scored suggestively below chance for ON targets and suggestively above chance for the -1 displacement targets. Thus the ESP mechanism, rather than disappearing, seems to have had its focusing distorted by the increased stress of the Training Study. Some preliminary studies by Lila Gatlin of the transinformation function, an information theory measure of relationship between targets and calls, suggest that in general there was a distortion of the ESP process for four of these five non-significant subjects. These analyses may be presented in a future publication.

TCT—Learning. The fourth and fifth columns of table 8 present the overall slopes and the mean within-session slopes for the TCT subjects. For the group as a whole, the mean overall slope is zero, and no individual slope is significantly different from zero. As with the Aquarius results, this provides moderate support for the learning theory application in that there is no decline effect (extinction) occurring, but the absence of any significantly positive overall slopes seems counter to the theory.

Inspection of the mean within-session slopes, however, shows some very positive slopes. The performance curves of the highest-scoring subject, S3, presented in figure 12, show that 8 of her 10 sessions had highly positive slopes, one a zero slope, and one a negative slope. If we take a null hypothesis that the probabilities of positive and negative sessions slopes occurring by chance are equal (ignoring the one zero slope), then the probability of eight of the nine slopes being positive is .002, 1-tailed, using the exact binomial distribution. Thus S3 learned to increase her ESP performance in almost all of her sessions, but lost most of this newly learned ability between sessions.

Examination of the intervals between sessions for S3 shows that they ranged from 1 to 29 days. There is a suggestive, but non-significant, rank order correlation coefficient of +.42 between the length of the intervals between sessions and the size of the inter-session performance drops. Future studies should minimize time lags between training sessions.

TCT—ESP Ability and Slope. In the Training Study, there is a correlation of +.66 between mean ESP score and slope (P < .05), as predicted by learning theory.[15] ESP scoring level on the TCT in the earlier Confirmation Study was also significantly related to slope in the Training Study ($r = +.71$, $P < .025$). In general, the more ESP a subject has, the more likely his performance curve will show an increase with practice.

TCT—Training Study vs. Selection and Confirmation Studies.   The same statistical considerations that automatically reduce calculated correlations even when true correlations might be high apply here, as they did for the Aquarius.

Taking mean hits/run in the Training Study as our main ESP measure, we find that mean hits/run in the Selection Study correlates $+.21$ ($N = 5$, non-significant) with it, and mean hits/run in the Confirmation Study (on the TCT) correlates $+.70$ ($N = 8$, $P < .05$, 1-tailed). If we use the best score on the TCT in the Confirmation Study as a rough measure of peak ESP ability, this correlates $+.27$ ($N = 10$, non-significant) with Training Study performance.[16] Thus there is some predictability of performance from the earlier studies, somewhat better than for the Aquarius. The better predictor here is mean performance, while the better predictor for the Aquarius was peak performance.

As with the Aquarius results, there was a suggestive drop in scoring level from the Confirmation Study to the Training Study. The results are presented in table 9 for the eight TCT subjects having all necessary data. The drop was in mean scoring rate, rather than in peak performance. With the exception of S3, the TCT

TABLE 9   **Scoring Rates on TCT, Confirmation and Training Studies**

	Confirmation Study	Training Study
Mean scores	4.78	3.85
	Pdiff $< .10$ (2-tailed)	
Best run scores	6.50	6.50
	ns	

subject who showed clear evidence of learning, the drop was, by inspection, spread equally between subjects who continued to show significant ESP abilities in the Training Study and those who did not.

TCT—Speed of Response. A number of experimenters thought their slower-working subjects tended to do best on the TCT. The best subject (S3, whose results are plotted in figure 12) generally took half an hour to an hour to do a single run of 25 on the TCT. In order to see if this relationship held in general, we used the mean number of runs done per session, since sessions were generally about an hour long, as a crude measure of speed for each subject. The rank order correlation coefficient between speed of response and the significance of overall scoring for each subject was -.62 (P < .05, 1-tailed). Thus slower subjects generally scored better.

TCT—Experimenter Difference. All five subjects who scored significantly for ON hits on the TCT were run by one experimenter, El, Gaines Thomas. His subjects had higher ESP ability to begin with, using Confirmation Study scores as criteria. They showed a mean performance of 5.45 hits versus 3.66 for the other subjects ($P_{diff} = .05$, 2-tailed, by t-test for independent samples) in the Confirmation Study. In terms of peak performance in the Confirmation Study, however, E1's subjects were not significantly better (mean best score of 6.6 versus 6.4). E1 was a very patient experimenter, whose subjects often worked very slowly.

Performance Differences on Aquarius and TCT. Far more ESP was exhibited by the subjects using the TCT than by those using the Aquarius in the Training Study. The probability of results on the TCT was 2×10^{-25}, while for the Aquarius it was 4×10^{-4}, considering the total groups of subjects using each machine. For the Aquarius this is about one genuine ESP response in addition to guessing about once every other run, while for the TCT we would estimate one genuine ESP response of a more difficult sort on every run. Thus there seems to be more than twice as much ESP manifested on the TCT as on the Aquarius.

Comparing results on the two training devices by significance level alone is misleading, however, for it is known that for a given amount of ESP operating, a test that uses a lower probability target will give a higher statistical significance than one that uses a higher probability target (Schmidt, 1970a). The psi-coefficient, described by Timm (1973), allows a comparison of effect per trial when target probabilities are different.

Computing psi-coefficients on those subjects who showed psi-hitting, the values for the Aquarius subjects range from .042 to .098, with a mean of .071, while for the TCT the values range from .066 to .164, with a mean of .100; so there was more ESP operating with the TCT.

Is the TCT a better device for eliciting and maintaining ESP than the Aquarius, or did it just happen that a more talented group of subjects chose to work with the TCT?

We can begin examining this question by comparing the Selection Study performance of the two groups of subjects. Those who finally trained on the Aquarius scored an average of 6.42 hits/run in the two-run Selection Study, while those who went on to train on the TCT scored an average of 6.60 hits/run. In terms of the best score from either run in the Selection Study, the Aquarius subjects averaged 7.42, and the TCT subjects 8.83. While the TCT subjects were slightly higher in each case, neither difference approached statistical significance. Note, however, that two runs per subject is a very insensitive measure that would reveal only very large differences in initial ESP talent.

If we take performance in the Confirmation Study as a more adequate measure of initial ESP ability of the two groups, and use scoring on the training device later selected by each subject in the Training Study as a measure of initial ESP talent, we find that the TCT group was definitely more talented. The Aquarius subjects totaled 392 hits versus 325 expected by chance, a highly significant performance ($P \approx 10^{-6}$) of an average of 7.53 hits/run, or 1.28 hits/run greater than would be expected by chance. The TCT subjects totaled 141 hits when 72.5 would be expected by chance ($P \approx 10^{-17}$), an average of 4.86 hits/run, or 2.36 hits/run above chance expectation. So in the Confirmation Study the TCT subjects are already showing about twice as much ESP per run as the Aquarius subjects *on the training device of their later choice.* In terms of psi-coefficients, the Aquarius subjects showed an effect of .069 per trial, while the TCT subjects showed one of .105 per trial.

It is important to emphasize that these performances were on the devices they later chose to work on in the Training Study, for strong differences appeared in performance on the two devices in the Confirmation Study. When tested on the Aquarius machine in the Confirmation Study, those subjects who later trained on it scored an average of 7.40 hits/run,[17] while those who later trained on the TCT scored an average of only 5.40 hits/run, a highly significant difference ($P < 5 \times 10^{-4}$). When tested on the TCT in the Confirmation Study, those who later trained on the Aquarius showed an average of 3.30 hits/run, while those who later trained on the TCT showed an average of 4.63 hits/run, a significant difference ($P < .025$). So although some subjects scored well on both devices, there was generally a strong difference. As mentioned earlier, there was a highly significant negative correlation ($r = -.69$) between performance on the two devices.

Because there was such a strong preference for one machine over the other, we cannot tell for certain whether the TCT group had more ESP talent to begin with, before starting the studies, or whether the TCT is a better training device. I am inclined toward the latter view, because in my opinion the four-choice set of the Aquarius gives too much misleading feedback (i.e., the subject is rewarded for being correct quite often when the correctness has been due to chance), and because of other differences between the machines discussed earlier, such as the experimenter/agent getting extra feedback on the subject's hand motions during his decision process.

Summary

The present procedure of serial selection for ESP ability in an ordinary student population, plus ESP training under conditions of immediate feedback, found 10 subjects (12 if the psi-missers are counted) showing individually significant ESP results. Six of them performed at significance levels of 10^{-4} and higher, one at the 10^{-23} level. The very large amount of ESP found makes this one of the most successful ESP experiments ever done, and represents an amount of ESP that could lead to productive functional studies. No subjects showed significantly negative slopes, and two learned to perform better. This method offers promise of a new era in ESP research, based on high-level, reliable performance.

I have stressed the importance of experimenter-subject interaction in describing experimental procedure. The next chapter, by the most successful experimenter, Gaines Thomas, illustrates the style of experimenter-subject interaction more concretely than I have been able to do previously. It also suggests why Gaines Thomas was a more successful experimenter and it provides data about the performance styles and experiences of the more successful subjects.

5 Training Subjects on the Ten-Choice Trainer
by Gaines Thomas

During my initial contact with each subject at the beginning of the Training Study, the following topics were covered:

1. I gave a complete explanation of the phased testing, referring to the earlier Selection and Confirmation Studies as screening procedures and to the Training Study as the actual experiment, from which they would not be disqualified.

2. I pointed out assumptions that we made in reference to ESP and this experiment, namely (a) that everybody probably has ESP, but the ability and/or the amount that could be demonstrated on our tests was highly variable within a population; (b) that in our tests we could not accurately discriminate among telepathy and clairvoyance, possibly not even precognition or, even more extreme, psychokinesis; and (c) that demonstration of ESP would be based on their beating chance as much as possible.

3. The purpose of the experiment was to determine whether ESP ability could be increased through practice and feedback.

4. We would work on the machine of their preference for the duration of the experiment.

5. The experiment would consist of 20 runs of 25 trials each.

6. We would try to set regular hours for testing, each test to be from one to two hours in duration or until one of us tired.

7. Since ESP is severely affected by distractions, if they should feel unwell, tired, under pressure because of tests, personal problems, etc., or just unwilling to participate on any given day, they should let me know by phone or note ahead of time and it would

be all right. In fact, I would prefer to cancel our appointment if they were not wholehearted about it.

8. I gave them a general rundown on the equipment, how it works, use of random number generators, etc. I stressed that numbers were random, and that it must be kept in mind that the same numbers may come up repeatedly and shouldn't be overlooked.

9. Before each session they could ask me any questions, cancel the appointment, give me suggestions, complaints, etc. Also I indicated to them that I'd be interested in hearing about any experiences they had that might be related to ESP, including what reactions they got from other people who found out that they were being tested for ESP.

10. The speed at which we would do each run would be dependent on them, unless they were so fast that I could not keep up with them.

11. After each run, I would indicate to them how well they did, how close they came, and ask how they made their decisions. We would also discuss how I concentrate on numbers and how they would like me to focus my attention (i.e., on the panel, the TV monitor, on the random number generator, or with my eyes closed). In the case of the Aquarius, this could be a matter of color, position, or figure; on the TCT, a matter of number or position.

12. I would indicate to them various processes I would like them to try, based on their sucesses and how they made their choices.

Based on what I observed when I was doing runs at the same time other experimenters were doing them also, and what the subjects of other experimenters told me, I found that my techniques differed in the following ways:

1. I spent more time with the subjects before runs and between them, discussing their results.

2. Initially I did *not* suggest any process for them to follow (i.e., hot-cold, strongest feeling, "electric" charge, etc.) in making their selections.

3. Once subjects were able to discriminate between hits and misses to some degree, based on some feeling or strategy *they* had developed, I began to have them experiment with one process at a time for a run or two, making changes depending on their degree of success. In the case of the TCT, this involved characteristics

(tendencies) of the choices they made—such as being one off to the right or left, hand movements (such as initial placement of a hand on the board before going around the circle of buttons and being often over the right number), or when two numbers stood out—and working with the criteria they used to make their decisions.

4. I made a strong effort to schedule times that were convenient for the subjects, at times of the day when they felt most alert and comfortable.

5. I made attempts to remind subjects by telephone about their appointments throughout the experiment.

6. At the end of each run, in the case of the TCT, I lit up all of the lights except the correct one, as a signal to them that the run was completed and that I would be with them in a few minutes, instead of leaving them hanging, expecting a green light to come on shortly.

7. I traded places with most of my subjects for one or two runs to make each of us more familiar with the other's position and feelings. These, of course, did not count as part of the 20 runs but occurred as monotony breakers approximately halfway through them.

8. I attempted to indicate to the subjects what methods (concentration methods) I could use on the sending unit. I then asked them which method or methods they would prefer me to use and generally followed their instructions, unless I became uncomfortable or I thought their performance was suffering.

9. I arrived about ten minutes early for each appointment so that I could have the machines plugged in and warmed up, ready to go as soon as the subjects arrived. This included taking care of the paperwork, so that I could spend the maximum of time with the subject without any distractions and so that there was a minimum of delay between the time I left the subject and the moment I began sending (unless the subject requested a specific delay to relax and begin his concentration).

10. I took a neutral attitude as far as my own beliefs were concerned. I stressed the fact that no matter how well the subjects did, there was always a possibility that chance was responsible, although evidence for the phenomenon was getting greater. I preferred to refer to ESP as a "phenomenon," as opposed to using

the initials, since some of my subjects were cynical about ESP but were more accepting of themselves as exhibiting a "phenomenon."

11. I differed from the other experimenters in the impression I gave my subjects as to my idea of an acceptable score. Although I told the subjects that their scores would form a normal curve if their ability was actually due to chance alone, I personally felt that any score below six (on the TCT) was not significant to me, nor would scores at chance levels be significant. All of my subjects picked up my personal standards. They became unhappy if they scored at chance levels, below chance, or only one or two above, although I am certain that at no time did I overtly degrade their scores or demand that they do better. However, I am also certain that they could detect if I was either disheartened or very pleased about their scores, so I believe these expectations played an important part in the performance of my subjects.

These standards were reinforced by having the probability of each score posted on the wall in the form of a table, within view of all the subjects. Also, my expectations changed as the experiment progressed. At the beginning I was looking for chance and slightly higher performance, but as subjects improved and the setting up of processes became fruitful, my concept of a good run increased in relation to their scores. It also appeared to me that their own concept of a good score increased.

Comments on Individual Subjects

S1 became involved mostly out of curiosity. He was my only subject who didn't go through Selection Study testing. After the Confirmation Study, he took a course in Transcendental Meditation, which made me curious as to whether or not his scores would improve as a result of it. I didn't note any difference and neither did he, despite his having 5- to 20-minute meditation periods immediately before each test session, which practice we later dropped.

He approached the testing more as a curiosity than as a scientific undertaking, although he expressed great interest in knowing about our procedures and the eventual results. His process was a fundamental one. He chose the number that seemed strongest to him. He had difficulty though, in trying to keep himself from falling prey to strategies, trying to outguess the random number generator. He characteristically would do three runs per session in the beginning, the first being poor, the second good, and the third poor again. Consequently, to keep himself from getting depressed, he later preferred to do only two runs a session. It generally worked; his scores averaged higher and he wasn't as disheartened, but he never thought, nor did I, that his scores were significant overall.

S1's performance is graphed in figure 13. He scored 78 ON hits instead of the expected 50, $P = 4x10^{-5}$, with an essentially zero (.02) overall slope. He showed significant spatial displacement on the -1 hits ($P < .05$), with his displacement hits (shown in the upper curve) for ON plus±1 hits generally paralleling the ON hit curve, suggesting a relatively constant distortion of the ESP focusing mechanism.

S2 is what I call a "spacey chick." You could never really know where her mind was at any given time. She characterized her technique as seeing vectors of light between various numbers on the board. I had her point out her "vectors" as she saw them before making a choice. She pointed them out in order of their coming to mind. They seemed pretty random, but quite often the first number she pointed out was right, or one off in either direction. She was very moody, causing me to cancel a number of appointments due to her feeling tired or tense, or she would forget to come to the appointment. She gave the impression of silently accepting the idea that she had some ESP ability, and she seemed rather enthused about the experiment. Seldom did her hits correlate with her feelings of "strong choices."

S2 scored 80 ON hits, $P = 8x10^{-6}$, with an essentially zero overall slope (-.02). She also displaced considerably both to left (-1) and right (+1) of the target, with the -1 displacement being independently significant ($P < .02$). Her performance is plotted in figure 14. As with S1, the ON hits and ON plus ±1 hits curves are generally parallel, suggesting a constant distortion of the ESP mechanism.

Of all my subjects, S3 was my star, my highest scorer. She was also unique in that she was by far the slowest. On the TCT, she

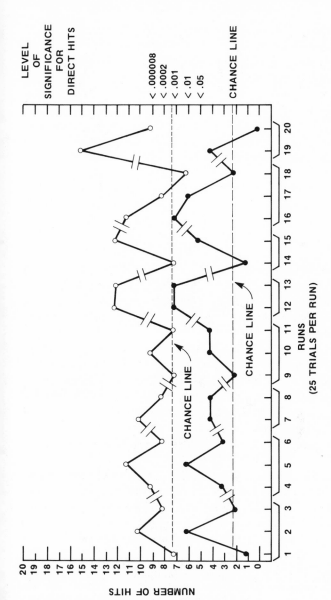

Fig. 13. Performance of S1, computer plot

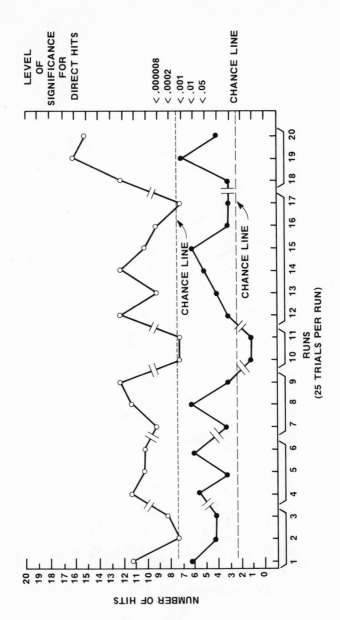

Fig. 14. Performance of S2, computer plot

would take about 45 minutes to complete one run. She was also the most absentminded. I would have to phone the night before and also the morning of the experiment to remind her. If I forgot to call, she would forget to come. A number of times she forgot to come despite my calling. She was also my only "handsy"-type subject on the TCT, meaning she used her hands to scan the numbers. Last, but most important, S3's best scores were attained by use of an extensive process which consisted of a number of steps:

1. Starting wherever she wanted, she would go around the circle, one number at a time, pausing as long as she wished. She'd say the number silently to herself at each position.

2. She would pull back, pause, and then place her hand over the number or numbers that had stood out most to her when she originally went around.

3. Two or three numbers would usually stand out to her in varying degrees of strength. Initially she chose the strongest, but after some experimenting with her process of decision-making, we determined that her scores were better if she chose the most recessive of the group that initially stood out after her scan.

4. Her scores were consistently better if she stayed with the recessive choice. When she varied from it in a few runs, her scores went down.

Through the use of the TV monitor, I noticed a few interesting characteristics associated with her hand movements. Often the button she began her initial sweep from was the correct choice. Also, after the first sweep, the place she went back to after pulling back and pausing was also quite likely to be the correct answer. I also noticed a tendency for her to change the position of her fingers as she went around the unit. When going around on the right side, her fingers and thumb would be close together. Yet, when she passed over the correct choice, her small finger would separate from the others, pointing outwards. This same phenomenon occurred on the left side, except it would be the thumb instead of the little finger separating. This didn't occur consistently, but I noticed it many times. If the other fingers became separated, there was no correlation.

S3 became very emotional when she chose the wrong one of her group of standouts. Other misses were simply dismissed. Many times she'd go back and forth between two or three numbers until she could discriminate the strengths between them. She was always very excited about the experiment, and would continue on if I was persistent about reminding her of the testing times. She always was surprised at how well she did, and she has had some phenomenal things happen outside of the experiment.

S3's performance graph was presented earlier in figure 12 (page 77). She made 124 ON hits when 50 were expected by chance, $P = 4 \times 10^{-28}$. Although her displacement hits were not independently significant, the occasional divergence of the two curves in figure 12 suggests that there may have been occasional difficulty with the spatial focusing of her ESP abilities.

The regression line for ON hits is also shown, in figure 12, as it is quite positive, even if not reaching statistical significance. S3's mean within session slope was $+1.90$, and she seemed to show a quite consistent pattern, discussed earlier, of learning within sessions but dropping during the long intervals between them.

S4 was my fastest subject. She was the only one I had to slow down by not setting the TCT until I had time to concentrate on the number. As soon as I set the machine, she'd respond within a few seconds by going directly to her selection in a quick, jerky manner. The most businessslike of all my subjects, S4 seemed to be a silent skeptic who showed amusement at her relatively high scores but became noticeably tired and bored in response to chance or lower scores. She did her best when she had one number that stood out in her mind. If she had two numbers, she attempted to make a choice based on which number had the most emphasis to her. Overall, she left the impression of being very conscientious. Her hits stood out very definitely to her.

She scored 81 ON hits, $P = 4 \times 10^{-6}$, with an essentially zero overall slope ($-.01$). Her ESP ability seemed sharply focused, with no significant displacements: the significance of the ON plus ± 1 hits curve comes almost exclusively from the ON hits. Her performance is graphed in figure 15.

S5 was my convert. Of all my subjects, she was by far the most cynical in the beginning. She answered negatively all of the

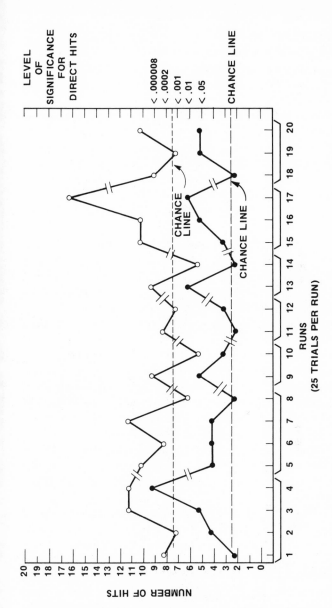

Fig. 15. Performance of S4, computer plot

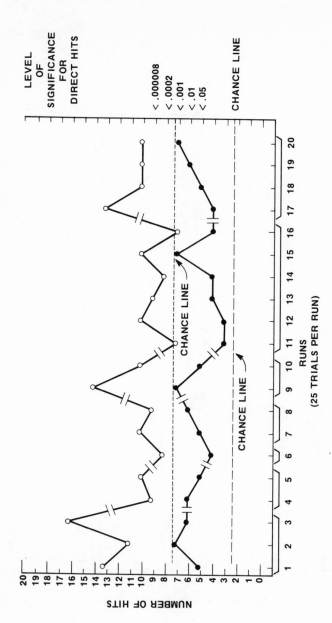

Fig. 16. Performance of S5, computer plot

questions on the Selection Study questionnaire, including the one regarding participation in the experiment. To get her in, I had to persuade her that if she did participate and her performance showed that she didn't have ESP, then it would verify her own concept that she didn't have any ability and would indicate either that our selection techniques were not effective or that ESP doesn't exist. This argument appealed to her, and she agreed to participate.

When I brought her in for Confirmation Study testing, I was surprised to find her more cynical than I had expected. She was blunt in her criticism, not failing to mention that she was pressed for time, didn't believe in ESP, and wanted to hurry and get it over with. The first day she did two runs, scoring a 5 and an 8 on the TCT. This shocked her visibly, but she didn't say anything and maintained her coolness.

I didn't see her again until after the Thanksgiving vacation. When she came back her attitude was completely different; she wanted to know all she could about ESP, the experiment, etc. She was very enthusiastic and cheerful. When I pointed out that she was a different person from the one I had seen, she displayed some agreement. I then asked her if she had talked to anyone about the experiment. She answered that she had told her family. Her father was pessimistic, but curious. Her mother was very enthusiastic and interested. Her brother and sister had been involved in some simple experiments in their elementary and junior high schools and were excited over her involvement. With that encouragement, she approached the experiment from a new perspective from then on.

Her scores were consistently above chance. Her process was simply determining which number was strongest in her mind and pushing the button. It would take her about 10 to 15 seconds to make a decision. She noticed some correlation between the feeling of a hit and correct guesses. Even now, though, I have the feeling that she doesn't believe in a phenomenon of some sort, but attributes her scores to chance.

S5 scored 103 ON hits instead of the 50 expected by chance, $P = 2 \times 10^{-14}$. Her performance is graphed in figure 16. The performance slope for her ON hits was essentially zero (−.03). She scored suggestively low (44/50) on −1 hits and suggestively high (57/50) on

+1 hits, but not significantly so. Her displacement performance seems more erratic than her ON performance, suggesting some erraticism in focusing the ESP mechanism.

The Sending Process

Lastly, I want to say something about my own methods of concentration. My normal procedure on the TCT was to push the button on the random number generator right after the subject had made his choice on the preceding trial and I had switched off the selection and recorded his choice. I then entered the new target number on the score sheet and silently repeated the number to myself, attempting to position it in my mind in a fashion that I can only describe as keeping it just "posterior to the upper part of my ears." Success very often correlated with a numbing feeling in that location. Once I felt I had the number positioned, I would turn on the proper target switch (which activated the Ready Light on the subject's console). I would then stare at the number (card) on the TV monitor until the subject made his choice, all the while maintaining the number in the same location of my brain. Sometimes I would orally coax the image on the screen, or swear at the near misses. In relation to the Aquarius, I preferred to focus on the color, which I felt centered in my forehead somewhere for best results.

Recommendations

1. Duration of the experiment should be set over a far longer period of time (four to six months at least).

2. "Processes" (strategies) should be worked out ahead of time, and then remain constant if possible during the actual experiment.

3. More attention should be paid to the subject's mood and to standardizing the periods for runs (i.e., regular appointment dates and times).

4. A set number of runs per session that is comfortable for both experimenter and subject should be determined ahead of time and maintained for the duration of the experiment.

5. The same experimenter-subject pairs should be maintained throughout the experiment.

6. More stress should be placed on informal discussions and feedback between experimenter and subject before, in between, and after runs.

7. Since many subjects seemed to avoid certain numbers on the TCT because they were hard to reach or out of their normal visual range, tilting the panel should be considered.

8. It would be helpful, in the case of the Aquarius, to have a switch to signal the subjects when the experimenter is ready for them to make a choice.

9. It might also be helpful, with the Aquarius, to have a TV monitor to give more feedback and process determination.

10. Academic credit should be given to subjects, if possible, for the large amount of time invested.

6 Discussion and Conclusions:
ESP Ability Can Be Trained

 Surveying the pilot study, main study, and other relevant studies in the literature, we may now draw some conclusions about the validity of my application of learning theory to ESP. We shall deal with the main predictions of the theory first, and then discuss various other points.

Prediction—Feedback Will Stabilize ESP Performance

Since repeated guessing without feedback constitutes an extinction procedure according to the theory, provision of immediate feedback should generally eliminate the usual decline effect, at least for short- to moderate-length experiments where boredom and loss of motivation do not become major problems. This is a minimal prediction about the effects of immediate feedback, but an important one, given the near universality of the decline effect (Pratt, 1949).

Table 10 summarizes the present studies and all recent studies by others that were reviewed in chapter 2.[1] Our attention here belongs in the third column. In 13 studies where slope data on individual subjects were available,[2] for a total of 227 subjects (studies 1, 2, 3, 4, 6, 7A, 12, 13, 17, 7B, 25, 27, and 28), there is only one significantly negative slope (decline), and that in a subject who showed no overall ESP ability (study 25). In 3 further studies (studies 18, 19, and 20) with another 34 subjects, 30 of them showed an increase in the proportion of correct confidence calls after feedback training, although we cannot evaluate whether these were significant on an individual subject basis. The other studies do not present relevant data on individual subject performance, although they reinforce the impression of steady, non-declining performance. Altogether, 256 of 261 subjects failed to show any significant decline (extinction) effect, and only one of the remaining 5 subjects definitely showed a significant decline.

There is little doubt that this prediction is confirmed: an application of immediate feedback eliminates the usual decline effect. This is the strongest finding of the present and other studies.

Prediction—Feedback Can Produce Learning of ESP

All of the studies presented in table 10 are consistent with this prediction, although the bottom seven are only trivially consistent since there was no clear manifestation of ESP in them.

For the 13 studies where relevant individual subject data are available, at least 15 of the 227 subjects showed learning; possibly more did, but this was difficult to evaluate in some subjects in the Tart and Redington main study. For studies 18, 19, and 20, 30 of the 34 subjects showed increases in their proportions of correct confidence calls, although the significance of these increases cannot be evaluated for each subject individually. Four other studies showed significant increases in ESP scoring for the group as a whole, even though we have no individual subject data, and three more showed increases in scoring, even though the increases were not statistically significant. Only one (study 24) found no ESP at all and no improvement for feedback.

In the first six studies where individual subjects clearly showed learning, they also showed very high amounts of ESP. Insofar as these subjects can continue scoring at these levels, much less continue to increase with further training, they are the "parapsychological batteries" we need.

Prediction—Greater ESP Ability Facilitates Learning

In the original presentation of the learning theory application, I noted that since the repeated guessing tasks become boring, because there is confusion caused by reinforcements for hits that are actually

TABLE 10 Studies of Feedback and ESP

Study	Number of Subjects[a]	Significant Negative Slopes?	Results Supporting Learning Theory Application
			Studies with Highly Talented Subjects
1. Tart, pilot study	10	No	1 subject may have learned; but great conflict
2. Tart & Redington, main study	25	No	2 subjects showed clear learning; perhaps more
3. Targ & Hurt, 1972	12	No	1 subject learned clairvoyance and precognition
4. Kelly & Kanthamani, 1972	1	No	1 subject showed clear learning
5A. Schmidt & Pantas, 1972 (study 2)	1	not calculated	
6. Kanthamani & Kelly, 1974	1	No	1 subject learned rapidly then fell off to steady, high scoring
7A. Targ et al., 1974 (Phase O)	1	No	1 subject clearly learned ESP
8. Ojha, 1964b	10	not calculated	Group showed very high improvement
			Studies with Mildly Talented Subjects
9. Mercer, 1967	20	not calculated	Group with feedback scored significantly; non-feedback group scored at chance
10. Dagle, 1968b	12	No	Feedback following non-feedback raised scores; reverse order kept scores high
11A. Fouts, 1973 (study 1)[b]	1	No	1 subject showed significant ESP with feedback
11B. Fouts, 1973 (study 2)[b]	41	not calculated	Group showed significant improvement with feedback
12. Sanford & Keil, 1975	1	No	Suggestive + performance slope, significant ESP hitting in one condition
13. Schmidt, 1969a	4	No	Steady ESP over 16,000 trials
14. Schmidt, 1969b	6	not calculated	Significant performance
15. Haraldsson, 1970 (main study)	11	not calculated	Full feedback better than partial feedback

16. Lewis & Schmeidler, 1971	14	not calculated	Scores insignificantly higher with feedback
17. Honorton, 1971b	1	No	Learning, but erratic
5B. Schmidt & Pantas, 1972 (study 1)	214	not calculated	Increase, but non-significant
18. Honorton, 1970	10	not calculated	9 of 10 subjects increased rate of correct confidence calls; significant increase in hitting
19. Honorton, 1971a	10	not calculated	8 of 10 subjects increased rate of correct confidence calls
20. McCallam & Honorton, 1973	14	not calculated	13 of 14 subjects increased rate of correct confidence calls; significant increase in hitting
21. Kreiman & Ivnisky, 1973	15	not calculated	Significant increase in hitting for group
7B. Targ et al., 1974 (all phases)	146	No	6 subjects showed significantly positive slopes

Studies with Apparently Untalented Subjects

22. Beloff, 1969	40	not calculated	No significant hitting
23. Banham, 1970	22	not calculated	Increase in scoring, but overall score not significant
24. Banham, 1973	30	not calculated	Decline effect for group, but overall score not significant
25. Beloff & Bate, 1971	4	1	3 subjects with positive slopes, one significant decline, no significant overall ESP
26. Drucker & Drewes, 1976	50	not calculated	Higher-IQ children significantly improved over 2 runs
27. Jampolsky & Haight, 1975	20	No	No significant hitting; 1 child showed significantly positive slope
28. Thouless, 1971	1	No	Perhaps learning with subsequent decline; overall score not significant

[a] Number of subjects who were run under immediate feedback conditions, not the total number used in the study.
[b] Study has methodological flaws, so results should be considered only tentative.

caused by chance, etc., we have a dynamic conflict between the learning potential and the extinction process. Thus I postulated a "talent threshold," some necessary minimal level of ESP ability on starting the learning task. Below this threshold, the process of extinction would be stronger, so even though immediate feedback would be expected to slow it, extinction would eventually predominate. Above the threshold, learning would predominate.

Note that the talent threshold is not a fixed entity. For a given talent level, higher motivation, higher general learning ability, etc., might shift the balance toward continued learning. For a higher talent level, we could tolerate less motivation, etc.

On a statistical level, ignoring possible non-linearity, this becomes a prediction of a positive correlation between ESP ability (scoring above chance expectation) and the slope of the regression line fitted to the performance curve.

Table 11 presents all relevant data.

TABLE 11 **Correlations Between ESP Ability and Slope**

Study		Correlation	Significance Level (1-tailed)
Tart, pilot study		+.10	ns
Tart, Training Study			
Aquarius:	TS slope vs. TS mean	+.35	ns
	TS slope vs. CS mean	-.29	ns
	TS slope vs. CS TCT mean	+.44	.10
TCT:	TS slope vs. TS mean	+.62	.05
	TS slope vs. CS mean	+.71	.025
	TS slope vs. CS Aq. mean	-.49	ns
Targ, Cole, & Puthoff			
Aquarius:	Phase II slope vs. mean	-.29	ns
	Phase III slope vs. mean, without outstanding subject	+.91	.005
	Phase III slope vs. mean, with outstanding subject	+.68	.05

Note: TS = Training Study, CS = Confirmation Study, TCT = Ten-Choice Trainer.

Recalling the statistical limitation that most of the calculated correlation coefficients are probably lower than true population values because of limited ranges of variation caused by the selection procedures in all these studies, we nevertheless see a good confirmation of the prediction. Seven of the 10 calculated coefficients are positive and 5 of these 7 are significantly different from zero; none of the negative coefficients is significantly different from zero. Thus greater learning is associated with higher ESP ability.

Estimating the Talent Threshold

Although there is no way known to me of predicting the approximate talent threshold for learning to predominate from the conventional psychological learning literature, we can now make a rough empirical estimate of it. If we accept that definite learning was shown by PS1 in the Tart pilot study, by S3 and S24 in the Tart and Redington study, by the subject in the Targ and Hurt (1972) study, by B.D. in the Kelly and Kanthamani (1972) and Kanthamani and Kelly (1974) studies, and by A2 in the Targ et al. Phase O study, we can calculate psi-coefficients for them of .145, .164, .098, .145, .139+ for B.D., and .073, respectively. This is a distribution generally quite higher than the range of .042 to .118 for subjects in the Tart and Redington Training Study who did not show learning, although there is some overlap, and a distribution range considerably higher than all the other studies with mildly talented subjects given in table 10, where psi-coefficients are generally less than .03 or so. This suggests that the talent threshold corresponds to a psi-coefficient of about .10 or so for an individual subject.

I emphasize that this is a rough calculation. Not only is it based on the very data in which learning occurred, which would boost the psi-coefficient, but it is based on subjects who were obviously successful in learning in relatively short training series. The threshold might be lower for well-motivated subjects willing to undergo long training. Certainly there is some suggestion of learning in less talented subjects on both the Aquarius and the TCT in the main study.

Length of Training

Inspection of individual performance curves in the Training Study shows that 20 training runs are not enough to adequately evaluate the full potential of the learning theory application. Most subjects were still showing high variability; none had reached a clear performance plateau.

The performance data are very much like those seen in biofeedback training, where a subject tries to acquire voluntary control over some normally uncontrollable bodily function, while getting immediate feedback on the state of that bodily function through instrumentation. Subjects will frequently start to show a rise in performance learning, then a major drop, often to below the level of the start of the learning curve. What happens is that they find a strategy that works to some degree, they get better at using it, but then they realize that this particular strategy takes them only so far; it's not the real answer, so they abandon it (showing a great drop in performance) in order to explore new strategies. The subjects in the Training Study were often doing the same thing, judging from their comments as well as their performance curves. They would improve a strategy that seemed to work, then realize it wasn't that good, or it wasn't continuing to show improvement, so they would drop it.

While there is little doubt that immediate feedback in talented subjects can eliminate declines and sometimes produce learning in short training efforts, the ultimate potential of the learning theory application must be tested in much longer studies. We can expect even greater improvements in performance than we have seen so far. It is also likely that we will obtain performance plateaus that will be long-lasting and difficult to surmount; once a person finds a very successful strategy for accomplishing a task, it is often psychologically difficult to handle the big drop in performance that comes from discarding that strategy in order to try something new.

Note that motivation will be a problem in longer studies. In the short studies the novelty of the task, the subject's interest in ESP, etc., make the immediate feedback on successful hits reinforcing. But as this novelty wears off, why should the subject continue working hard at a task which no longer seems so interesting? It may be necessary then to add external rewards for hitting.

Alternative Interpretations of the Results

I have interpreted the results of the present study and other studies as strongly supporting my original hypotheses, generated from applying elementary learning theory to repeated guessing processes in ESP, viz.: (1) immediate feedback can stabilize ESP performance; (2) immediate feedback can produce learning in some subjects; and (3) greater initial ESP ability produces more learning under immediate feedback conditions, i.e., some level of initial ESP talent is required for immediate feedback to be highly effective. I am aware that there are alternative explanations of the present data that do not consider immediate feedback a relevant factor. To briefly mention some:

1. The present good results came about through the serial selection procedure, locating subjects who were able to keep up their ESP for unknown reasons.

2. Feedback *might* be relevant, but it is a weak procedure to depend on the results of other studies which show that decline is well-nigh universal without feedback to act as an implicit control group. A no-feedback control group is needed.

3. Using California college students produced much better ESP results than older studies because these young students are in a new generation that is more open to ESP generally.

4. ESP performance stayed up because the experimenters maintained a close, friendly, supportive relationship with the subjects.

5. Because the experimenters believed that decline would be eliminated and learning could occur, it happened. That is, we are dealing with experimenter influence rather than with an effect of immediate feedback.

There is some merit in all of the above counter-hypotheses, at least in suggesting other variables which may be important in addition to immediate feedback. I shall not argue against them here, for my purpose in this book is not to say the final word on the learning approach, but to emphasize that it could be a key to reliable ESP performance, and to show that much evidence supports this idea. Any large, complex set of data can be interpreted in a variety of ways. I emphasize the learning interpretation to stimulate research that may be very important.

Finally I want to mention an alternative interpretation that is actually a *mis*interpretation and deserves emphasis, namely, that since most or all of our subjects did not show significantly positive slopes, immediate feedback does not produce learning of ESP ability. This misinterpretation comes from ignoring the qualifications of the original hypothesis presented in chapter 1. I do *not* hypothesize that any or all subjects can learn better ESP performance if they are given immediate feedback of results. Because of the "false" reinforcements in hitting by chance alone, a repeated guessing procedure is noisy and, to some extent, will always be an extinction procedure, *unless* a subject has a high enough initial ESP talent level for the learning process to predominate. The specific hypotheses, supported strongly by the data of the present study and others are as follows:

1. ESP performance will be stabilized by immediate feedback, i.e., the typical decline will be eliminated for short to moderate periods for subjects with some initial ESP.

2. *Some* subjects will show learning under immediate feedback conditions.

3. There will be a positive relationship between overall ESP ability and the slope of the learning curve. The more ESP you have to start with, the more chance of learning. A talent threshold was postulated, interacting with motivation and innate, general learning ability, as another way of stating this relationship.

In suggesting things to be considered in future research, I shall continue to interpret the results in terms of the learning approach, in order to be maximally provocative.

Suggestions for Further Research

Based on the findings of the Training Study, there are a number of tentative suggestions for guiding future research, in addition to the main conclusions drawn above.

First, the fact that at least some subjects may show sharp drops in ability between sessions should be taken into account. Whatever subtle cues are learned during a session that aid the ESP calling process may not be retained very well in memory. Thus we should probably move in the direction of long training sessions (but taking care not to cause fatigue and boredom) and short intervals between them.

Second, particular attention must be given to the talent threshold concept. If our main interest is to produce exceptionally high-scoring ESP subjects, we should follow serial selection techniques, as used in the present study, and devote our training efforts only to those subjects who show high ESP abilities to begin with. Given the limited manpower available to parapsychological research, this is probably the best course.

On the other hand, we need more information to estimate accurately the talent threshold and/or to determine how critical it is. This means giving extensive immediate feedback training to many subjects who span a wide range of initial ESP ability.

Third, we need more information on the threshold or level for the "experiential reality" of ESP, subjects' reactions to reaching this level, and ways of dealing with conflicts this may engender. Our discussion of pilot study subject PS1 is relevant here. This reality threshold is probably far more variable from subject to subject than is the talent threshold, for it will depend on the compatibility or incompatibility of ESP with individual belief systems, previous ESP experiences, etc. Some of the performance plateaus we can anticipate finding in extended feedback training may be actually resistances to reaching the reality threshold.

Fourth, I favor the ten-choice TCT over the four-choice Aquarius, for a variety of reasons. Comparison between the two trainers was not a major goal of the study, so I will comment only generally. My feeling is that a four-choice machine encourages guessing; there is too much hitting by chance alone, adding confusion and noise to the learning process. The ten-choice TCT moves toward the free-choice situation that White (1964) argued so cogently was the most effective for eliciting ESP. Perhaps even more choices would be useful, such as a 10×10 checkerboard arrangement.

The feedback to the experimenter/agent via the closed-circuit TV was probably also useful in teaching him to "send" better, although there is no way of formally testing this hypothesis in the present study. It certainly kept each experimenter/agent psychologically involved in his role.

The finding that slower speeds of response on the TCT led to generally higher scores is also important. Some subjects working with the Aquarius reported that when they weren't doing well in a run they just dashed through the rest of it in order to finish. While this may have helped them to express their feelings, it defeats the whole purpose of giving immediate feedback, at least in terms of *conscious* learning where we expect a person to note the kinds of feelings he has just before making a guess, note whether the guess is successful or unsuccessful, and keep mental notes on the optimal strategies that emerge from this. Subjects could not dash through a run on the TCT to the extent that they could on the Aquarius because there was always a delay of a few seconds while the experimenter recorded the previous response and set up the new target. Perhaps a modification of the Aquarius so that the experimenter has to set up the next target remotely (now available as an option from the manufacturer) would be advantageous.

Note, however, that while I think a ten-choice task is better than a four-choice one, this preference must be modified to match the subject's preference, or we sap motivation.

Finally, I want to emphasize that my application of learning theory to ESP performance is an elementary one, made while I was still a graduate student. I am not an expert in learning theory. But given how well this elementary application has worked out, where might a sophisticated application take us? Suppose, for example, we took into account the multiple-step nature of the ESP process (Tart, 1973b) in order to provide a more complex type of feedback that would be more informative to the subject? We shall do this a little in the next chapter.

I hope the future will see more sophisticated experimentation here, for I am confident that the learning theory application may give us our parapsychological batteries. Even at the elementary level of the present study, exceptionally significant amounts of ESP were steadily manifested in an ordinary, college-student population.

7   **Inside the Mind:**
Further Theoretical Considerations

Traditional learning theory methods have been behavioristic—approaches where you measure and talk about inputs to a person and his behavioral responses without theorizing about what goes on inside him. My initial formulation of the learning theory application was guided by what data I had on how people felt about ESP experiences as well as by traditional learning theory. However, I stayed with the input-output method in order to communicate effectively with colleagues who had been schooled in that approach, and have largely kept that style throughout this book. In this chapter I shall theorize about internal mental processes involved in learning to use ESP, and shall suggest some other lines for future research.

A Model of Telepathy

Why is ESP so unreliable? I think we can get a partial answer to this question by modeling the phenomenon and noting the sheer complexity of it.

Figure 17 is a relatively straightfoward model of telepathic transmission, adapted from some earlier work of mine (Tart, 1966c), where one person, the agent, or sender, looks at a target and tries to mentally send it to a subject, or receiver. By definition, we eliminate all possible means of sending the information that can involve sensory stimulation of the subject. The subject eventually gives us some behavorial response which, when compared to the target, convinces us that information was indeed transferred.

Imagine a horizontal line one-third of the way up, separating the boxes labeled *encoding, channel,* and *decoding* from the rest of the figure. The processes below this line are the *para*psychological aspects of telepathy. The processes above the line are probably all psychological processes. Let's look at the parapsychological aspects of this model first.

The process I've labeled *encoding* is a mysterious but necessary process to account for the fact that while the message seems to reach the receiver, the patterns of neural impulses—the form in which it exists in the sender— do not cross any useful amount of space. If you put a person into an extremely expensive, ultrashielded room, and use the very best modern equipment, you can pick up electrical or magnetic components of neural activity up to a few centimeters away, but they disappear into the noise level of your instruments after that. Take away your fantastically expensive shielding and you're wasting your time trying to pick up any electrical or magnetic components of neural activity even a centimeter away from the skin. So encoding is a process we need to hypothesize to convert these patterns of neural impulses into whatever unknown form of energy it is that can cross space and reach the receiver in spite of barriers that shield out known forms of energy. The message is encoded from neural patterns into some unknown form of energy. At present we have no idea what the organ for telepathic encoding might be.

Any kind of information gets from one location to another by going over some kind of channel, just as the air serves as a channel for the sound waves of someone's voice reaching you to stimulate your hearing. Although we don't have any very systematic research on it, my best guess at this time would be that the channel for telepathy to operate over is just space. *Space* is an easy word to throw around, but it is more a concept we take for granted than anything we really know much about. When I ask my physicist friends what space is, they just tell me it is too fundamental a conceptual category to be defined! Since ESP has been shown to work through large amounts of physical shielding (Vasiliev, 1963) and over vast distances, including one successful experiment by the astronaut Edgar Mitchell (1971), while he was orbiting the earth and the other half of the team was on the ground, "just space" is all we can say about the channel's nature at this moment.

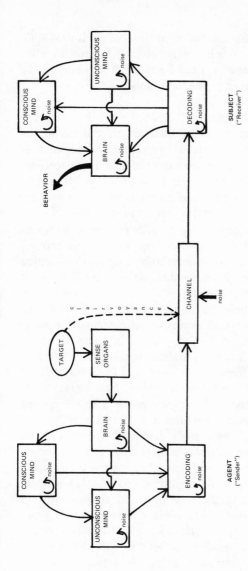

Fig. 17. A model of the telepathy (GESP) process

While our ignorance about the nature of the channel is profound, we do know something else quite important about it, namely, that like every other channel we know of it can be noisy. This noise can be divided into random noise and systematic noise.

Noise

Random noise, the aspect we know least about, consists of the irrelevant and conflicting energy put out by hundreds or thousands or millions of other people in between the sender and the receiver, particularly in experiments done over long distances. It is preposterous to assume that only the one person in the world who has been designated as a sender is putting out whatever energy conveys ESP at that particular time, and yet the message gets through, as successful experiments have shown. The decoding process in the receiver is obviously enormously selective in order to pick up only the desired message. How it cuts through the random noise of all these other minds is a total mystery at present.

We know a little more about systematic noise in the overall system and channel from several recent experiments. Systematic noise is noise which will uniformly distort the signal in some direction, rather than just randomly lowering the signal to noise ratio. The first study was carried out by Honorton, Ramsey, and Cabibbo (1975) at the Maimonides Medical Center in Brooklyn, New York. Many informal observations in parapsychological research had suggested that the quality of experimenter-subject interaction influenced results, so they tested this hypothesis explicitly by running two groups (18 subjects per group), tested individually, under positively or negatively toned interaction conditions. The positive group had a 15-minute casual, friendly, and supportive conversation with an experimenter before starting the ESP task and received further encouraging comments during the testing. The negative group started the task immediately, and the interaction was structured to be formal, abrupt, and somewhat unfriendly, with discouraging comments on subjects' performance during the testing.

The experimental task was predicting which of two indicator lamps would light when a trials button was pressed. The lamps were being alternately selected one million times per second to insure that the selection produced by the trials button was random.

Subjects receiving the positive interaction treatment scored 1,867 hits when only 1,800 were expected by chance (P < .02), while subjects receiving the negative treatment scored significantly *below* chance (psi-missing), with only 1,721 hits instead of 1,800 (P < .01). Thus the experimenters' style of interaction introduced systematic noise into the process, although in this study we can conceptualize the noise as entering through sensory channels and perhaps operating in a conventional manner on psychological processes rather than affecting transmission in the ESP channel per se. The study is also a clear demonstration of how the presence of hostile skeptics during an ESP experiment may obliterate the phenomenon.

I stress the importance of experimenter effects, for in almost all psychological and parapsychological experiments there is someone around, usually the investigator, who strongly desires to see the results come out in a certain way. As psychologists we have long worked with a now obsolete concept taken from nineteenth-century physics, that of the *detached observer* who has no effect on what he observes. Orne's work on demand characteristics (1962) and Rosenthal's work on experimenter bias (1966), as well as studies by myself and others (Troffer & Tart, 1964), should lay this myth to rest. I believe it is now much sounder experimental procedure *always* to assume that the experimenter may be inadvertently and subtly affecting the results unless it can be otherwise proved.

Can't this kind of bias be controlled by careful regulation of experimenter-subject interaction? Maybe. But another study indicates that systematic bias, noise, can occur by ESP over the channel.

Kreitler and Kreitler (1972) had various student subjects come in for several conventional psychological procedures. One was measuring tachistoscopic thresholds for the recognition of words. A second involved the autokinetic effect, where subjects watched a pinpoint of light in a dark room and had to report when it appeared to move either left or right, even though the light was actually fixed. The third involved the subjects' making up stories from TAT-type cards. Unbeknown to the subjects, experimenters in distant rooms, who had no direct contact with the subjects and who did not believe in ESP (at least consciously), deliberately tried to influence them telepathically. The experimenters would try to lower the recognition threshold for selected words in the tachistoscopic experiment, try to increase the proportion of autokinetic movements in a certain direction in that experiment, and try to make certain kinds of thematic material appear more frequently for particular TAT cards. It could be inferred that, by deliberately using experimenters who did not believe in ESP, Kreitler and Kreitler were trying to prove that experimenter bias could not be transferred telepathically in ordinary psychological experiments. Nevertheless, all three studies showed that the skeptical experimenters definitely influenced the subjects' responses telepathically. The Kreitlers' results have been independently replicated by Lübke and Rohr (1975).

How much more bias might occur in an ordinary psychological experiment where, since the experimenter has no idea he might be using telepathy, he needn't waste energy in conflicts about it, and because of a strong emotional investment in having the data come out in a certain way, he has emotional energy available to help activate the telepathic process?

This is a disturbing question, and I suspect that for a long while we shall deal with it by the traditional ostrich technique of burying our heads in the sand and forgetting all about it. But eventually we must face it. Meanwhile the data have a very immediate application in attempting to make ESP phenomena more reliable. We must account for the beliefs and desires of the experimenters and observers as well as those of the subjects in ESP experiments. This is why I have described the experimenter-subject interaction at length in chapter 4 and have included Gaines Thomas' comments in chapter 5.

Other Aspects of the Model

Continuing with our model, I am using a telepathy model here to fully illustrate the complexities in ESP. However, note that this also becomes a clairvoyance model (the direct perception of the state of physical events without the information existing in another mind) through the insertion of the dotted arrow in figure 17 that is labeled *clairvoyance*. Here information flows directly from the target into the channel, and so on into the subject. Note also that this becomes a model for precognitive telepathy and precognitive clairvoyance if we "simply" allow the channel to extend forward in time as well as through space. Simple of course to describe, but quite another thing to make any real sense of! While we have excellent evidence for the reality of precognition, I personally have very conservative ideas about time and cannot begin to understand precognition, so I will simply note that we can model it this way and move on.

Finally we come to the last step of the *para*psychological process—the decoding process, or the receptor for ESP. Again, we must hypothesize a receptor for this unknown form of energy which transforms it to neural impulses, but we really have no idea what the receptor is at the present stage of our knowledge.

Now look above our imaginary horizontal line and consider the psychological aspects of the process. We have a variety of scattered bits and pieces of psychological knowledge about psychological processes going on in ESP—far from a complete picture, but enough to indicate that these are probably similar to other kinds of known psychological processes. Let's look at the receiver first, where we have most of our scattered data, as senders have been rather neglected in research.

The Receiver

I distinguish here our conscious mind to indicate our direct experiences, the unconscious mind to include Freudian and other kinds of unconscious processes, and the brain and nervous system as the final processor of outputs from both these systems before they eventuate in some kind of behavior that is our final output. We can conceive of, and find evidence to support, four possible information flow routes from the decoding process to behavior.

The simplest is directly from the decoding process to the brain and nervous system, eventuating in some kind of measurable behavior. This is the sort of flow that occurred, for instance, in an experiment I carried out almost 15 years ago (Tart, 1963), in which a subject was monitored for physiological responses while a sender in a distant room received a painful electric shock at random intervals. The subjects showed autonomic and EEG activation patterns at the time of the shock as if they had been receiving a mild sensory stimulus, yet their conscious guesses as to when they thought something might have happened showed absolutely no relationship to the shock occurrence times.

The second information flow route is from the decoding process to consciousness to the brain and nervous system to behavior. This is the "simple" route that we tend to think of automatically; our "ESP organ," whatever that is, gets the message, we are aware of it, and we then express it. I had a personal experience of this sort many years go when trying to act as a receiver for a well-known psychic. In general I did quite miserably, scoring at chance level, but once when he was attempting to send a target, I suddenly had a vivid visual image of a sailboat flash into my mind and that was the target picture he was holding in his hand. The image was striking because it had an alien feel to it; it didn't seem like my style of visual imagery at all. Unfortunately, this simple information flow route seems to operate quite rarely in most subjects. We don't know how to get in contact directly with the decoding process.

The third information flow route is from the decoding process through the unconscious mind to the brain and nervous system and then to behavior. An example of this might be ESP expressed through automatic writing. The subject will have no idea of what his hand is going to write next, and, consciously, he can be carrying on a totally unrelated conversation. Yet along with much rambling and many irrelevancies, ESP sometimes comes through, frequently with the kinds of transformations and distortions we associate with unconscious processes.

Finally, we can picture a flow route from the decoding process to the unconscious mind, which then sends a transformed version of the information to the conscious mind, the information then being expressed through the brain for our final behavior. An excellent example of this is Gertrude Schmeidler's sheep-goat effect (Schmeidler & McConnell, 1958), where believers in ESP, the sheep, tend to score *above* chance expectation on card guessing tests, thus confirming their belief that they have ESP. The nonbelievers, the goats, tend to score significantly *below* chance expectation, for by doing poorly on the test they believe they are confirming their belief that there is no ESP. But there is only one way they can score significantly below chance: on some trials they must unconsciously use ESP to guess the correct identity of the target, and then the unconscious must influence the conscious mind to be sure it makes a *wrong* guess.

The Sender

To glance briefly at the sending side of the process, the neglected half of the telepathic team, we can again picture four possible information flow routes, although we know much less about the actual operation of each. We start in all cases with an information flow route from the target through the appropriate sense organ for perceiving it to the brain and nervous system. From there we might have a route directly to the encoder, whereby the information is sent without the agent's knowing it. Or we might have what seems the obvious route, to consciousness and then to the encoder. Unfortunately, since the agent generally does not know how to send other than just to wish it would happen, a more likely route is from consciousness to the unconscious mind and thence to the encoder, where the wish is translated into action. We also could conceive of a route directly from the unconscious to the encoder.

Within every one of these processes, both in the sender and in the receiver, I have indicated the existence of noise—random noise, as in being preoccupied with irrelevant things, as well as systematic noise that might help or hinder the process.

By this time it is probably clear that the telepathic process is complicated, and that understandably it does not work very reliably or strongly! That is exactly the impression I have tried to convey. If we think, for instance, of the simplest information flow route in this simplified model, from target to sense organ to brain to encoder to channel to decoder to brain to behavior, it involves eight separate processes. Assuming no significant noise sources in the target, or in the sender's sense organs, or in the final behavioral expression by the receiver, that gives us five possible noise sources. And there is no guarantee that the simplest route is used. The reality may be that the most complex route is used, which would be from target to sense organ to brain to consciousness to unconscious to encoder to channel to decoder to unconscious to consciousness to brain to behavior, twelve sequential steps with at least nine possible noise sources. It seems a wonder that ESP works at all!

The Learning Theory Application

There are similar complex processes that we use in ordinary sensory communication, and these work quite successfully because we have immediate feedback information on how well our systems are working and thus can constantly adjust them. If you hear yourself use a phrase that fails to convey the meaning you want, you can stop and use another phrase or explain yourself.

The application of learning theory to the ESP process as described in this book is a recognition that ESP is probably a complex, multi-step process, like ordinary sensory communication, and that it needs immediate feedback to give the people involved the opportunity to "tune up" their systems, to learn the internal feelings associated with good and poor ESP performance and adjust their functioning accordingly.

Our model of the ESP process will change now with the addition of immediate feedback, and this is shown in figure 18. Here the target identity goes into an external feedback control mechanism, in this case something that will hold the identity of the target until after the receiver has made his behavioral response, and will then feed the information about the target back to the receiver via his sense organs and brain and nervous system and so on into his mental processes. You will also note a second feedback arrow, namely, feedback on the receiver's behavior back to the sender, so that he can learn something about the most effective ways of sending. This will include the specific important aspect of the receiver's behavior, what particular response button he pushes, and, for the TCT training setup, nonspecifics, such as his general hand movements over the target response console. Now we have feedback so that the complex system may make adjustments for optimal information transfer.

Note again that this is a GESP model. To the extent that the agent/sender is important, the feedback to him is of value in helping

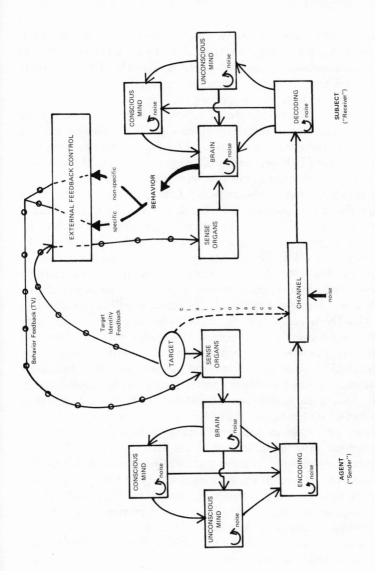

FIG. 18. Adding immediate feedback to the telepathy (GESP) process

him to send more effectively. To the extent that the subject is clairvoyantly perceiving the targets, only the immediate feedback to him is important, and the feedback to the agent/sender may act only as a motivator to keep him interested in what is going on.

In terms of the results supporting the learning theory application, reported in an earlier chapter, I believe some of the subjects were indeed successful in "tuning up" their systems, in getting some idea of what kinds of momentary states of feeling, effort, etc., went with good and poor ESP performance. I do not believe any of them came near peak performance, but they were off to a good start.

I plan to do considerable work in following up these results, and I hope that others will too. A replication of this series of studies is planned, which will include a much more complex ESP trainer that will allow greater convenience and sophistication in studying the scoring patterns. So far this has been a very simple application of learning theory to the ESP process; with the aid of learning theorists, much more sophisticated applications can be made.

My own future expansion of this research will try to take into account the overall *state* of the receiver and the sender as well as the simple correctness or incorrectness of response outcome. Figure 19 shows our telepathy model again, but this time with the addition of physiological recordings from the subject, coupled through a computer-operated feedback control system. This would not only use physiological responses as indicators of ESP per se, as in one of my earlier studies (Tart, 1963), but it would try to keep track of various physiological parameters of the subject and how they correspond with the efficiency of the ESP process, and would eventually start giving feedback signals to a subject to the effect that he is or is not in a condition associated with good ESP performance. If he is, then obviously he should respond; if not, he should wait for a change or deliberately try to alter his condition. The subject's physiological data could also be fed back to the sender so that he could have a chance to learn what kinds of sending efforts have optimal matches to various subject states.

Nor should we neglect the role of the experiment/sender in this processs. Figure 20 shows that we can also monitor behavioral and physiological responses of the sender, run them through an

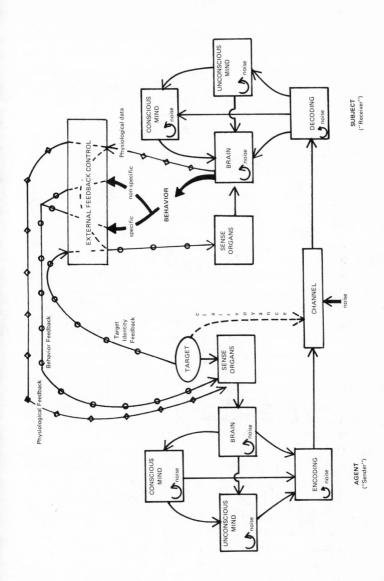

FIG. 19.   Telepathy model with physiological recordings of and feedback to subject

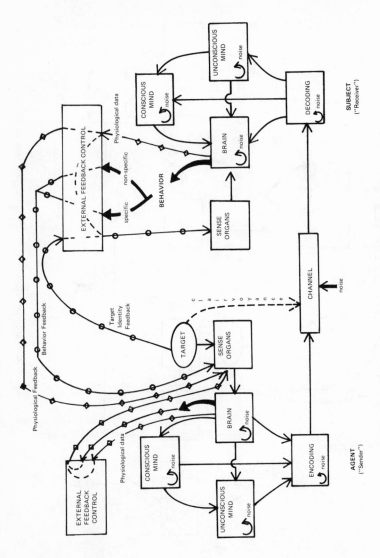

FIG. 20. Telepathy model with physiological recordings of and feedback to sender

appropriate computer system to learn what kinds of behavioral and physiological conditions on the agent's part are associated with successful sending, and eventually give the sender such feedback so that he can improve his sending. The possibilities I see here are quite exciting. I leave it to the reader to think of further ones.

In practically all learning situations, a subject receives almost immediate feedback as to whether he was correct or incorrect in his response. His performance then improves with practice. To extinguish a learned response, or to keep it from being learned in the first place, no feedback is given.

In the typical ESP testing procedure, results are not known to a subject until the end of many trials: the run. This delays feedback so long that, from the point of view of learning theory, there is little or no effective feedback. The decline effect, a falloff in performance with practice, is well-nigh universal in published studies of ESP and supports this analysis of the typical repeated guesses/no feedback procedure as one of extinction.

When you are right by chance alone a certain proportion of the time, the situation is more complicated, for you are rewarded for irrelevant guessing rather than for using ESP. If a subject has no ESP ability to begin with, immediate feedback should have no effect. If he has a little ESP, immediate feedback should stabilize performance and slow extinction, but the confusion/noise generated by chance reinforcement may eventually bring about extinction. If the subject has ESP ability above a critical "talent threshold," the learning process should predominate. The talent threshold is not absolute, but interacts with motivational level and overall learning ability.

Given subjects with some ESP ability, three formal predictions follow from this analysis:

1. Immediate feedback of results will stabilize ESP performance, eliminating decline/extinction effects for short- to moderate-length experiments.

2. *Some* subjects will show increasing performance with repeated practice under conditions of immediate feedback.

3. The greater a subject's ESP abilities, the more improvement is expected.

This theory is spelled out in detail in chapter 1.

A number of experiments have appeared in the literature which support the learning theory application. They are reviewed in chapter 2.

A pilot study, reported in chapter 3, demonstrated the feasibility of equipment for supplying immediate feedback, showed results indicative of ESP, and showed that the learning theory application must be modified if unconsciously motivated psi-missing occurs.

The major test of the theory was a three-phase study reported in chapter 4. Since subjects with ESP ability were needed to adequately test the learning theory application, the first two phases of experimentation were for selection purposes, the Selection Study and the Confirmation Study. Significant amounts of ESP were found in both. Most subjects went through the studies serially if they showed individually significant ESP ability in each, while a few skipped one study. Twenty-five subjects graduated to the main study, the Training Study, in which they carried out 20 runs of 25 trials each with immediate feedback. Fifteen subjects worked throughout with the four-choice Aquarius trainer, 10 with the Ten Choice Trainer.

Both final groups showed highly significant ESP results, especially on the TCT. The predictions stemming from the learning theory application received strong support, namely:

1. ESP performance was stabilized; there were no significant declines within the Training Study.

2. One subject showed a significant increase on the four-choice trainer for overall performance, while others showed patterns of increases within training sessions (several runs), but falloffs in performance between runs, so some subjects did show learning.

3. Slope of the overall performance curve was positively related to

degree of ESP ability, although the correlations did not always reach statistical significance.

Reports of the more successful subjects' mental processes and their ESP performances are presented in chapter 5.

The Training Study results are combined with those of other investigators' studies in the discussion in chapter 6 to show that the predictions of the learning theory application have received excellent support from some 200 + subjects. Additionally, a rough estimate of the talent threshold, above which the learning process outweighs the extinction inherent in repeated guessing, was made. The threshold estimated is a psi-coefficient of about .10 for a given subject.

A more theoretical look at the internal mental processes involved in ESP, as well as the importance of immediate feedback to allow both senders and receivers to optimally adjust themselves, is presented in chapter 7.

The magnitude of ESP obtained in the present study was very high, enough to allow productive functional studies of the nature of ESP. Parapsychology has been plagued by intermittent, unreliable, low-level ESP manifestations that have made functional studies very difficult. It is hoped that the present procedures may offer a key to practically significant and reliable ESP performance, and thus warrant extensive research.

The Ten-Choice Trainer

The Ten-Choice Trainer (TCT) was originally built for use in the pilot study reported in chapter 3. At that time there was no grant support available for the research, so the construction of the TCT presented a dual challenge: to build a training device that was technically adequate, and to do it by scrounging the kinds of surplus parts that would be lying around unused in most psychology department shops. The resulting machine met the challenge: it can be built for a hundred dollars or less (through shopping for parts on the surplus market) by any technician with a basic knowledge of electricity and simple hand tools. Some specific improvements can be made, which will be discussed here. Also, Dana Redington and I are designing a far more sophisticated TCT for use in future research. However, the present design should do quite well for others who wish to start work in this area.

The TCT has been designed for a ten-target guessing situation, but may easily be adapted to any number of targets from two upward.

Randomization and target selection can be accomplished in the traditional fashion of the experimenter thoroughly shuffling a target deck of appropriate symbols. This should be a subdeck culled from a much larger deck in order to keep it open. This deck then determines the order in which switches will be closed by the experimenter throughout the experiment. We switched to the random number generator shown in figure 9, chapter 4, part way through our main study.

For a given trial, the experimenter turns up a card and closes the appropriate Target Selection Switch on his console. This simultaneously lights a pilot lamp beside that switch (with the target symbol next to it), giving the experimenter a fixation point if he is attempting to send telepathically, and lights a Ready Light on the Subject's Console, informing the subject that a target is being sent and he may guess when he is ready. The panel layout is shown in figure 8, chapter 4.

The subject makes his choice by pushing the appropriate button on his console. The Subject's Console is laid out to be almost identical to the Experimenter's Console, and is shown in figure 7. Pushing the button: (1) activates the Trials Counter on the Experimenter's Console to increase this count by one; and (2) activates the Hits Counter on the Experimenter's Console if the subject's guess was correct. If the Feedback Control Switch is in the Off position, nothing further happens. If it is in the All Trials position, the correct lamp, the one the subject *should* have guessed, lights on the Subject's Console, giving him complete feedback on the target. If the Feedback Control Switch is in the Hits Only position, the correct lamp comes on only if the subject guesses correctly. A chime in the Subject's Console will also automatically sound on hits if it is switched on at the Experimenter's Console.

The experimenter then opens the Target Selection Switch, cutting off all lamps on both panels, and goes on to select the next target card and repeat the above procedure. The mechanics of selecting the card and activating the machine take only about two seconds after practice, longer if the experimenter makes notes of targets and responses. The subject may respond as rapidly or as slowly as he desires once the Ready Light comes on.

The Subject's Console also contains a Pass Button; if the subject does not want to guess on a given trial he may press this, signaling the experimenter, who can then select a new target. The Pass Counter records this, but neither the Trials nor the Hits Counter is activated, and the subject receives no feedback on what the passed target was.

The Experimenter's and Subject's Consoles are interconnected by multiple-conductor cable, which may be several hundred feet in length. Low voltage is used for safety. Cable lengths of up to several thousand feet may be used with large cable.

Let us now consider the electrical operation of the TCT in detail.

Target Setup

Figure 21 presents the circuit (except for a power supply) of the TCT. We shall trace the operation of the circuit by assuming that Target #2 has been selected.

When the power is initially turned on, no lamps light and no current flows anywhere in the apparatus. Then the experimenter closes Target Selection Switch #2 (S-2), and several things happen. Consider them from the top contact on down.

First, Target Lamp #2, the experimenter's fixation point, is connected in parallel with Lamp #2 on the Subject's Console. Neither lamp lights yet.

Second, the common Hit Line in the Experimenter's Console is connected to a contact of Relay #2 of the Subject's Console, but, as Relay #2 is open, no current flows. No voltage exists in the common Hit Line unless the subject presses Button #2 (thus closing Relay #2), an event we shall consider below.

Third, voltage is applied from the + Power Bus to the experimenter's Target Lamp #2, which lights. The corresponding lamp on the Subject's Console does not light because the Feedback Relay (Subject's Console) is open.

Fourth, voltage is applied from the + Power Bus to the Ready Line, lighting the Ready Light on the Subject's Console, informing him that he may guess.

The above four actions are, of course, simultaneous, since all four poles of the switch close together, but they were looked at sequentially for the sake of analysis.

Subject Responds Incorrectly

Let us assume that the subject responds incorrectly by pushing Button #1 (B-1) on his console. This closes two separate sets of contacts on Relay #1. The upper set applies voltage from the Ready Line to the individual Hit Line for Target #1, but as this contact in Target Selection Switch #1 on the Experimenter's Console is open, it does nothing. The lower set applies voltage from the Ready Line to the Trials Line. This voltage does two things: first, it activates the Trials Counter to increase the count by one; second, it goes to the Feedback Control Switch.

Subject's Panel

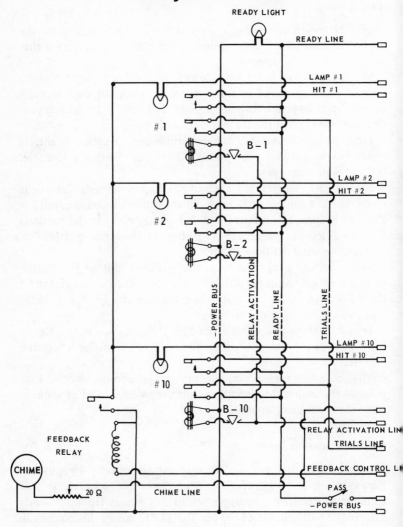

FIG. 21a.   Circuit of the basic Ten-Choice Trainer (subject's panel)

Experimenter's Panel

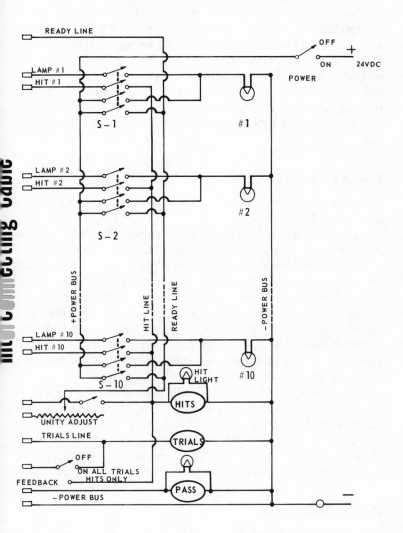

FIG. 21b. Circuit of the basic Ten-Choice Trainer (experimenter's panel)

If the Feedback Control Switch is in the Off position, nothing happens, and the subject receives no feedback on the correctness or incorrectness of his guess. If the Switch is in the All Trials positon, as it was for all studies reported herein, voltage is applied to the Feedback Control Line and activates the Feedback Relay. Its contacts complete the circuit for the lamps on the Subject's Console, and whichever lamp was chosen as target (#2 in this case) will light, showing the subject that he should have guessed #2 instead of #1. If the switch is in the Hits Only position, nothing will happen on this trial.

Subject Responds Correctly

Let us now assume that the subject correctly pushes Button #2 (B-2), rather than #1.

The Trials Line will be activated by the closure of Relay #2, just as in the case of an incorrect response. The voltage applied to the individual Hit Line for Target #2 now, however, finds a closed contact in Target Selection Switch #2 on the Experimenter's Console, and so activates the common Hit Line. This causes the Hit Counter to advance one, lights a Hit Light on the Experimenter's Console (designed to reinforce the experimenter), and, if the Feedback Control Switch is in the Hits Only or All Trials position, activates the Feedback Relay so that Lamp #2 on the Subject's Console lights, informing the subject that he was correct.

Another switch connected to the Hits Counter goes to the Chime Line. If this switch is closed, a door chime of pleasant tone will sound in the Subject's Console. Subjects report that they value the sound of this chime very much. Use an ordinary door chime with about a 20-ohm, 24-watt adjustable resistor to make it operate satisfactorily on the 24 volts of direct current used in the apparatus.

Physical Construction

Construction is straightforward and may be adapted to a particular investigator's requirements. My apparatus consists of two almost identical panels. On each there are 10 switches (or buttons) arranged in a circle about 18 inches in diameter. A pilot lamp lies just outside each switch or button. Thus targets may be identified by a number (1-10), a position (top, 30°, etc.), or a symbol (playing cards) placed beside the lamp and switch.

The Subject's Console is completely enclosed to prevent tampering with the circuit.

The Experimenter's Console also contains a Power Switch, counters for Trials, Hits, and Passes, a Feedback Control Switch, a Hit Light, and a Pass signal lamp. (A duplicate Ready Light is in the center of the circle on the Experimenter's Console to further make the panels physically alike, but its function is redundant in this case.)

Fraud-proofing

What if a subject pushes several buttons simultaneously, to increase his chances of a hit?

The variable resistor, labeled *Unity Adjust* in figure 21, makes this impossible. It is in series with the voltage (obtained from the Ready Line) needed to operate the relays in the Subject's Console. It is adjusted so that only enough current can flow to close one relay at a time. Thus, if the subject pushes several buttons, one will almost always be pushed a fraction of a second before another, and only that relay will close. If a subject managed to push two or more buttons exactly simultaneously, no relays would close.

The value of the Unity Adjust resistor should be determined empirically, based on the particular relays you use. Connect a variable resistor in series with a relay coil and switch; adjust it just above the point where the relay will close when the switch is activated. Connect a second relay coil in parallel with the first, to ascertain that voltage cannot now close both relays.

Another possible source of error occurs when lever action switches are used for the Target Selection Switches. If these switches are pushed rather slowly, some of them will make contact irregularly, which could cause the Ready Light to blink before coming on steadily. Quick, regular selection and switch pushing by the experimenter eliminates this problem.

Note that it is possible for a deliberately cheating experimenter, or one with unconscious response patterns, to transmit cues that the subject could pick up. For example, if the experimenter always hesitated longer between trials when the cards called for Target #1 to be chosen, the subject could learn that this long delay was associated with that target. Again, quick and regular action by the experimenter seems to eliminate this problem, and we found no empirical support for it in our main study. An alternative would be to install a timing circuit in the power line, such that the interval between trials was fixed and always long enough for the experimenter to have completed the selection process, an improvement that I shall use in future experiments but which will automatically slow down the rate at which the subject could respond.

Components

I have deliberately refrained from putting part numbers on the components, so that the experimenter may adapt the circuit to whatever parts he can obtain. Many surplus components, at very low prices, can provide all the necessary parts. Some general comments do apply, however.

First, use low-voltage components for safety. I have used 24 volts direct current because of its wide availability in many psychological laboratories.

Second, select lamp sizes that are not too bright for comfort. Small pilot lamps can be very irritating to look at if they are too bright or in an inadequately shielded fixture.[1]

Third, be careful not to get the "make before break" type of switch, as this can cause the circuit to malfunction.

This completes the description of the basic apparatus, which has been successfully used and "debugged." Several improvements that have since been added to the apparatus and were used in all the studies discussed earlier will now be described.

Self-Contained Power Supply

For those not having access to 24 volts direct current, a simple power supply is shown in figure 22. Using an 18-volt secondary on the transformer, a bridge rectifier, and a single, large filter capacitor will provide 24 volts direct current. It is poorly regulated, but regulation is not important in the basic circuit. The transformer secondary need supply only an ampere or two, unless you use very low resistance relays. The chime draws several amperes on hits, but that is only a momentary load.

Total Feedback to Experimenter-Agent

The basic circuit only tells the experimenter whether the subject has guessed correctly or incorrectly on any given trial. If the experimenter is trying to learn how to "send," and/or wants to note individual responses, he needs to know exactly which button the subject pushes on each trial. A simple modification of each Target Selection Switch on the Experimenter's Console will accomplish this, as is shown in figure 23, with the modified wiring shown as a heavier line.

Instead of the four-pole single-throw switches shown in figure 21, four-pole double-throw switches are used. When a target has not been selected, the pole connected to the individual Hit line from the Subject's Console is not simply off, but is connected to the corresponding lamp on the Experimenter's Console. If the subject pushes that button, the corresponding lamp on the Experimenter's Console will light. All other aspects of circuit operation are identical. The closed-circuit TV feedback, described in chapter 4, also gives the experimenter more opportunity to learn to send.

Response-Locking

In the basic TCT (with or without the modification for giving total feedback to the experimenter), the various scoring and feedback circuits are active only so long as the subject continues to hold his response button down. If the subject just jabs at the button, this may be enough to activate the Trial and Hit Counters, but the brief blink of the panel lamps may not provide adequate feedback. Also, if the experimenter wants to keep a record of individual responses,

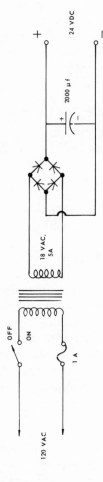

EXPERIMENTER'S PANEL

Fig. 22.   Simple power supply for the Ten-Choice Trainer

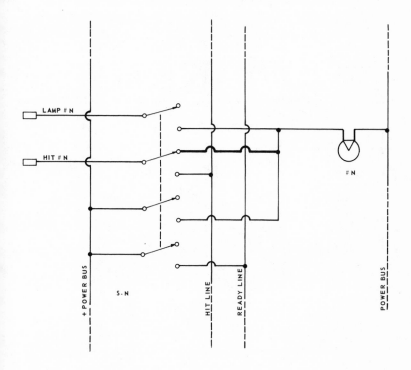

Fig. 23.   Modifying the Ten-Choice Trainer to give feedback to the agent-sender on the subject's choice

SUBJECT'S PANEL

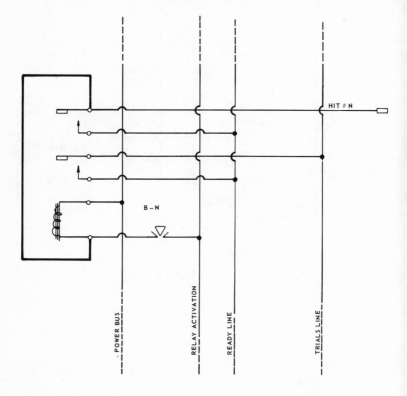

Fig. 24.   Modification to the Ten-Choice Trainer for Response-locking. After a subject presses the button of his choice, the selected target lamps (target and response) remain on until the experimenter opens the selection switch.

rather than just total scores, he cannot do so under these circumstances.

The heavy line in figure 24 shows a modification, made to each relay, that locks the relay closed as soon as the subject pushes his button. Even though the subject removes his finger, the relay stays closed for that trial on the Experimenter's Console. Thus the experimenter has as much time as he needs between trials.

Electrically, this works, because as the upper relay contacts close, the voltage from the Ready Line is thus connected to the relay coil, in parallel with the voltage applied through the button. When the button is released, current still flows through the Ready Line, locking the relay. Note that this effectively disables the Unity Adjust control. But, if the modification for total feedback to the experimenter has been incorporated, this does not matter, because several lamps on the Experimenter's Console would come on if the subject pushed several buttons, and the trial would be discounted.

ESPATESTER:
*An Automatic Testing
Device for Parapsychological
Research*

More than three decades ago, J. B. Rhine (1939) pointed out the need for automatic equipment in carrying out tests for extrasensory perception (ESP), and W. Grey Walter (1965) more recently reaffirmed this need. G. N. M. Tyrrell (1936–37; 1938) had built one such device before the publication of Rhine's article, and a number of others have been designed or constructed since then (Cutten, 1961; Smith, et al, 1963; Stewart, 1959; Taves, 1939; Webster, 1949). To the author's knowledge, however, none of these devices is currently being used in parapsychological research.

Standard procedures used in testing for ESP involve: (1) randomly arranging cards or other target material by shuffling or by reference to tables of random numbers; (2) copying the guesses of the subject or having the subject himself write them down; and (3) hand-checking the subject's guesses against the actual order of the target material. This procedure is not only quite laborious, but it prevents the subject from working very rapidly; and, in order to guard against scoring errors, a perennial criticism raised by critics of parapsychology—see, e.g., Price (1955)—elaborate and time-consuming procedures of duplicate records, independent checkers, etc., are necessary (Humprey, 1948). A most important drawback of these standard procedures, however, is that they add a *constant* psychological condition to almost all ESP experiments, viz., that the experimenter is rather busy and cannot devote his full attention to the subject during the testing. Since this is an experimental con-

Reprinted from the *Journal of the American Society for Psychical Research*, 60 (1966): 256–69, by permission of the American Society for Psychical Research. I have updated a few passages.

dition that may influence the test results, it should be possible to vary it in order to assess its effect, and not have it always present whether we want it or not. Thus there is a definite need for a device which would accomplish three basic functions in order to free the experimenter for more profitable activities: (1) automatically generate random targets; (2) allow the subject to respond at whatever speed he desires, and not be concerned with record-keeping; and (3) make an objective record of the results. Additional desirable features have been discussed by Rhine (1939), and many of these will be mentioned in the discussion of the device proposed below.

Of considerably more potential importance than the convenience and safeguards against error that would be provided by an ESP testing machine, however, is the fact that only with automatic testing aids does it become feasible to use and investigate the effects of immediate reinforcement on ESP performance. As was discussed at length earlier (see chapter 1), standard card guessing tests probably constitute an *extinction* procedure rather than a *learning* procedure. This discussion pointed out that automated testing devices were required in order to provide the immediate rein-forcement necessary for learning. The device described in this appendix will extend the earlier discussion by illustrating how such an automatic testing device may be constructed.

In view of the need for a testing device, then, and the fact that several have been proposed and/or built in the last two decades, why are such devices not in common use today? There were a number of practical drawbacks, shared to various degrees by almost all of the previously proposed machines, which may explain why they are not currently in use. The chief drawbacks were: (1) lack of true randomicity in the generation of targets; (2) so much complexity that only highly trained technical personnel could construct and maintain the devices; (3) expense; (4) lack of sufficient flexibility to justify the expense and time involved in their construction and maintenance; (5) slow and cumbersome operation, most of them requiring the subject to push two or more buttons or levers on every trial; and (6) lack of portability. There were various other dis-advantages peculiar to individual machines.

The ESPATESTER

Following is a description of the construction and operation of a proposed device, ESPATESTER (*ESP* Automatic *TESTER*), which should satisfy the need for instrumental aids in ESP testing. First, the device will be described generally, and, second, a detailed technical description of its operation will be given.

The ESPATESTER performs two basic functions:

1. It automatically generates a randomly selected target within 50 milliseconds following the subject's previous response. This target may be an indicator light, the internal electronic state of the apparatus, an agent's perception of an indicator light, or any other sort of event which can be controlled electrically by the addition of accessory apparatus (slides, sounds, music, etc.).

2. It automatically scores each response of the subject as correct or incorrect, and on three electromechanical counters displays (a) the total number of trials, (b) the total number of hits, and (c) the total number of misses (this counter is optional).

The same outputs that provide scoring information may be used to operate information feedback devices or reinforcement devices.

The ESPATESTER has been designed around a line of behavioral programming equipment widely used in psychological research.[1] As will be explained in detail below, this has resulted in an extremely flexible device, for the ESPATESTER can readily be used with a wide selection of behavioral programming equipment, thus making many of the techniques developed in psychology in the last few decades readily adaptable to parapsychological research. It would have been possible to build all the units of the ESPATESTER from generally available electronic parts, but this would have resulted in no financial savings when all the extra time required was figured in, and it would have sacrificed the considerable advantage, discussed below, that the ESPATESTER may be constructed by most laymen.

The uses and advantages of the ESPATESTER are as follows:

1. ESPATESTER may be used for GESP tests by having an agent observe pilot lights indicating the target selected, or for "pure" clairvoyance tests by having no agent observe the indicators and having only the total trials and total hits indicated on the counters.

It may be used for precognition tests by having the target selection take place after the subject indicates his response (slight changes in the basic circuitry are made for precognition tests).

2. With some modification, ESPATESTER could be used for PK tests by asking the subject to attempt to influence the random selection process.

3. Because the target selection process is much faster than the highest speed at which a human subject can respond, the subject may respond as quickly or as slowly as he wishes. Pushing one button to indicate his selection is all that is required on each trial. The push buttons are all that the subject has on his console (except for optional reinforcement devices), so the machine is psychologically inconspicuous.

4. Cheating by the subject is virtually impossible. An electronically sophisticated subject, left alone with ESPATESTER for some time, might be able to cheat, but this contingency is easy to guard against.

5. With the addition of a polygraph, any or all of the following may be automatically recorded for *each trial*: (a) which target the machine selects; (b) which target the subject selects; and (c) a marker signal indicating the correctness or incorrectness of the subject's choice. The purpose of this latter signal is to even further reduce chances of scoring error when later going over the polygraph record. If either (a) and (b) or (a) and (c) are recorded, the following variables may be measured from the polygraph record for each trial: (a) the subject's reaction time, and (b) the length of time the subject held down his selector button.[2]

6. The problem of scoring errors by the experimenter is virtually eliminated with ESPATESTER, for the experimenter's only task is to write down the totals on the various counters at the end of each run. If a polygraph record is also taken, a completely objective record of the experiment is permanently available. It would be quite feasible to run subjects on ESPATESTER without the experimenter even being present.

7. ESPATESTER should be useful in studies attempting to find physiological correlates of ESP, because such physiological measures can be recorded on the same polygraph as the ESPATESTER

output, thus making a convenient and accurate record. Or they can be written out on two separate polygraphs to insure independent scoring. (Or part of one record may be masked during scoring.)

8. Most of ESPATESTER consists of standard, commercial modules that an intelligent layman (which is how the typical parapsychologist is classified when it comes to electronics) could plug together in a few hours (including mechanical assembly). The other units can be built by anyone who is able to use simple hand tools and solder.

9. Because ESPATESTER is mostly constructed of commercial, off-the-shelf units, troubleshooting and repair can be carried out by the layman by substituting units. The commercial units used have very high reliability, however, and malfunction should be rare.

10. ESPATESTER is very flexible. By adding other commercial modules made by the same company, many additional functions can be carried out. As a few examples: (a) the data on each trial can be punched directly on tape suitable for computer analyses; (b) rewards of various types (money, buzzers, pinball-machine-type displays) can be given to the subject on fixed or variable schedules with fixed or variable delays for correct responses; and (c) negative reinforcements (the nice word for punishments), such as electric shock, can be given on fixed or variable schedules after fixed or variable delays for mistakes. Such positive or negative reinforcement could be given to the agent as well as to the subject. A simple form of reinforcement could be carried out by simply mounting the hits and misses counters on the subject's console, giving him immediate knowledge of results on each trial.

11. By the addition of a few switches a novel experimental technique is feasible—the mixing of GESP and clairvoyance trials within a single run. Here the agent would know what the targets were on some trials but not on others (or some of the targets on all the trials) by having the experimenter disconnect some of the indicator lights. Other novel techniques could easily be programmed.

12. Auditory cues from the operation of ESPATESTER do not give away what target has been selected. It is almost completely silent in operation, except when the counters operate. Nevertheless, ESPATESTER is designed so that the subject's console may be

located remote from the device itself. The experimenter can use up to several miles of connecting cable to separate the subject from the apparatus. Remote placement of the indicator lights would also allow the agent to be situated at a considerable distance from the apparatus. It would even be possible (at extra expense) to develop a telemetering device to allow ESPATESTER to work over telephone lines, so the experimenter who really wants distance can conduct tests from one end of the earth to the other!

13. The whole device may be built in a large suitcase, allowing ESPATESTER to be taken into the field for investigation.

14. ESPATESTER is of very general use in the laboratory whenever random number sequences are desired. While this paper focuses on the parapsycholgical uses of ESPATESTER, its random generating section can be used separately in many areas of scientific research.

The cost of the components for the basic ESPATESTER is about $1,600,[3] not including a polygraph if this sort of record is desired. While this is somewhat high, it is within the reach of many parapsychologists. When compared to the freeing of their time for more productive experimentation instead of clerical work, it is an excellent bargain.

ESPATESTER was set up and checked by the author and found to operate quite satisfactorily. In addition, the Massey-Dickinson Company set up an automatically operated version of the random generator section of ESPATESTER and sent the results of over 300,000 trials to the author to analyze for randomicity. These data are represented in table 12, and indicate a satisfactory degree of randomicity for equal probability of target selection. Later, blocks of 1,000 targets each were tested for equal frequency of doublets and triplets by the Chi-square test, and showed no significant departures from randomicity.

We now turn to the technical description of ESPATESTER, which stresses principles of operation; many modifications could be introduced in collaboration with an electrical engineer. The particular circuit shown, however, is complete in itself, and this version of ESPATESTER can be built directly by any experimenter who has any proficiency with electrical circuits.

TABLE 12   **Frequency of Targets**

Cumulative Number of Selections	0	1	2	3	4	Mean
907	171	167	196	181	192	182
1,605	321	305	337	318	324	321
2,484	492	503	510	493	486	497
3,249	654	648	669	643	635	649
4,114	825	823	828	791	847	823
4,877	980	988	992	965	952	975
5,671	1,132	1,163	1,139	1,129	1,108	1,134
6,525	1,283	1,344	1,321	1,296	1,281	1,305
7,359	1,429	1,499	1,524	1,453	1,454	1,472
302,311	60,336	60,551	60,096	60,927	60,401	60,462

Circuit Of The ESPATESTER

ESPATESTER comprises two parts, the subject's console and the main unit. The subject's console consists of a box on which there are five push buttons and any reinforcement equipment desired, such as counters to indicate hits and trials, that may or may not be connected for a particular experiment.[4] The subject's console is placed in a different room from the main unit and from the agent (if one is used), in order to eliminate all problems of sensory leakage. A cable, of any desired length, connects the console with the main unit.

Operation of the ESPATESTER consists simply of turning on the power and telling the subject to start guessing. As the electronics equipment is all solid state, there is no "warm-up" time. A Ready Light can easily be added to perform this latter function, if desired.

A description of the component modules, which are transistorized units that plug into the main unit, is necessary for an understanding of the ESPATESTER. These modules will be described briefly here; a fuller description is given in the Massey-Dickinson catalog.

The Output Control is a transistor-driven relay. Two output control units are mounted on a single panel.

The Input Modifier-Delay is a device which provides a signal output of fixed duration once it is triggered. This output should be set to approximately 50-milliseconds' duration for ESPATESTER use.

The Electromechanical Counters count the number of input pulses delivered to them and display this count at all times.

An And Gate is a device which has two input "legs" and one output. It produces an output signal only as long as an input signal is present at *both* input legs simultaneously. (In figure 25, And Gates are represented by triangles, and "And" is represented by the ampersand symbol, &.)

An Or Gate produces an output signal as long as there is an input signal on *any one* of its input legs.

An And-Inhibit Gate is a device that produces an output if a signal is present at *one* of its input legs, but produces no output if a signal is present at the inhibit input leg. The latter signal "inhibits" the output.

The Counter-Stepper unit counts the number of input pulses coming into it by selecting a new output for each input, up to ten. In ESPATESTER applications, it is set so that on the fifth count it goes back to one and begins again. Thus a continuous train of input pulses makes the outputs cycle "around and around" a series of five positions.

On the Subject's Console are a set of five push buttons, controlling a series of DPDT relays with mercury wetted contacts.[5] These push buttons should be of the mechanically interlocked type, so that only one may be depressed at a time. Electrical interlocking could be substituted for mechanical interlocking.

The Lamp Driver is a multiple amplifier unit which makes an input signal strong enough to light a small lamp.

The circuit of ESPATESTER is shown in figure 25.

The operation of the ESPATESTER may be considered in terms of three functions: (1) the generation of targets; (2) the scoring of responses as correct or incorrect; and (3) the production of signals for external recording of targets and responses. These will be discussed in turn.

Generation of Targets

The targets are randomly generated as follows. One Output Control, shown in the upper left of figure 25, has its output fed back into its input, so that it oscillates at several hundred cycles per second, the exact frequency being determined by the mechanical inertia of the relay armature. Because of a mechanical factor, namely, the relay contacts bouncing as they hit each other, output pulses are actually produced at a rate of several thousand per second, on the *average*. These output pulses are quite variable in their timing and duration, and over a fixed time interval the total number varies randomly.

Such a fixed time interval, of 50 milliseconds (an arbitrary time), is produced by the Input Modifier-Delay unit. At the *end* of each response by the subject (when he releases a push button), a signal is generated on the Reset Line via an Or Gate which activates the Input Modifier-Delay unit. This 50-millisecond pulse is applied to one of the input legs of And Gate #6 (designated $\&_6$ on the diagram). The pulses from the oscillating Output Control are always being fed to the other input leg of And Gate #6, and so are allowed to reproduce themselves at the output And Gate #6 for 50 milliseconds.

Since each pulse advances the Counter-Stepper, and the total number of pulses per 50-millisecond interval varies randomly, the final position (and corresponding output) of the Counter-Stepper at the end of each 50-millisecond interval varies randomly. The outputs of the Counter-Stepper are connected to the Lamp Driver unit, so at the end of the interval one lamp lights, indicating at which position the Counter-Stepper has stopped. This lamp may be used to indicate to an agent in GESP tests what the target is, or it may be ignored or turned off for "pure" clairvoyance tests. This circuit is generally termed an electronic "roulette wheel," and is similar to the way the Rand Corporation (1955) produced its one million random digits.[6]

Scoring of Responses

The scoring of responses as hits or misses occurs as follows. Assume that on a particular trial the Counter-Stepper has stopped on position #3. Its output has activated one input leg of And Gate #3. Now assume that the subject incorrectly pushes button #1 (designated S1 on the diagram). This activates one input leg of And Gate #1 (via relay 1, designated RY1), but since its other input leg is not activated, no output results. Pushing button #1 also presents a signal to one input of the Or Gate, which in turn presents a signal

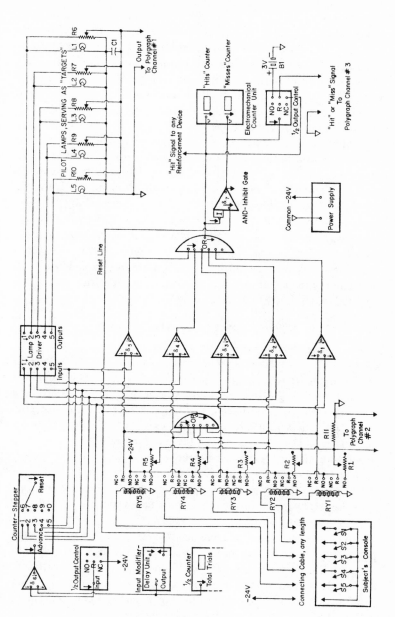

FIG. 25.   The circuit of ESPATESTER

to the And input of the And-Inhibit Gate, and since there is no input on the Inhibit leg of this gate, an output is produced which results in a count of one on the Misses Electromechanical Counter. When the subject releases his button, a new target is generated by the termination of the signal on the Reset Line, as described above, and the ESPATESTER is ready for the next trial.

Now suppose that the subject had correctly pressed button #3. This would have activated the other input leg of And Gate #3 and produced an output pulse which would pass through the second Or Gate and produce a count of one on the Hits Electromechanical Counter. This signal would also inhibit the And-Inhibit Gate, via the first Or Gate, blocking off the signal generated by all push buttons that would otherwise activate the Misses Electromechanical Counter. As before, the cessation of this latter signal from the push button (via the relay and first Or Gate) would activate the Input Modifier-Delay and set up a new target for the next trial. Each activation of the Input Modifier-Delay also produces a count of one on the Total Trials Electromechanical Counter.

Production of Signals for External Recording

The production of signals for external recording of trials and responses occurs as follows. When one of the five lamps has been lit by the Lamp Driver, indicating which target has been randomly selected, part of the voltage developed across the lamp is led to a polygraph channel, causing the pen to deflect a fixed distance, and to stay deflected until the subject makes a choice and releases his push botton. The voltages from all five lamps are fed into the same polygraph channel (via potentiometers R6–R10), but a different proportion of the voltage is taken from each lamp, so the height of the pen deflection depends on which lamp is lit. Five heights can easily be set, by means of the potentiometers in the lamp circuits, to be quite discrete visually.

Which button the subject presses may be recorded on a second polygraph channel. By means of the voltage dividing network composed of potentiometers R1 to R5 and resister R11, a different amplitude voltage is fed to the second polygraph channel, depending on which button is pressed. The polygraph pen will remain deflected until the subject releases the button.[7]

Each trial may be conveniently designated a hit or miss on a third polygraph channel.[8] If it is a hit, the signal going to the Hits Electromechanical Counter is fed directly out to the polygraph through the normally closed contacts on the Output Control (drawn in the lower right-hand corner). If the response is a miss, the signal going to the Misses Electromechanical Counter activates the Output Control and switches the polygraph input over to a fixed signal of opposite polarity and different amplitude, supplied by a battery. Both these signals cease when the subject releases his button.

Figure 26 illustrates how a polygraph record of three trials might look.[9] The top channel records the target selected, the middle channel which button the subject pressed, and the third channel whether the response was a hit or a miss. Although this information can be gathered by comparison of the first two channels, the presence of the third channel greatly reduces the possibility of scoring errors in reading the polygraph record, since only a much grosser discrimination is required.

Time interval t_1 is the time taken to set up a new target for each trial, viz., 50 milliseconds. Time t_2 is the reaction time between push button presses for the subject, and time t_3 is the length of time the subject holds down a button. In this particular hypothetical example, target #2 has been selected. The subject responds by pressing button #4 and holding it down for only 50 milliseconds (indicating a very brief jab at the button). This produces a Miss signal on the third channel. The ESPATESTER then selects target #5, the subject correctly presses button #5 500 milliseconds after his previous press, holding the button down for 100 milliseconds, and a Hit is registered on the third channel. The ESPATESTER then selects target #3, the subject presses button #1 450 milliseconds later, a Miss is indicated, etc. The subject's finger lingers on the button for almost half a second. The counters have meanwhile indicated a total of three trials, one hit and two misses.

Mechanically, all of the Massey-Dickinson module units are mounted by simply plugging them into rail units which contain the power connections. These rail units are designed to mount on standard 19-inch relay racks. Such a small rack could in turn be mounted in a suitcase. Signal connections and output connections among the units are made with patch cords having snap connectors

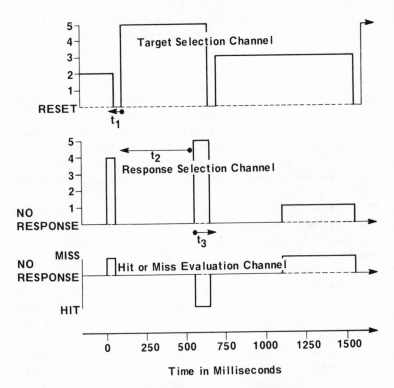

Fig. 26.   Polygraph record of three ESP trials

on the ends, so these interconnections are quite simple. The only soldering required is for the push buttons on the subject's console, the relay circuits, the voltage divider units, and the lamp sockets for the target lamps.

Randomicity in Target Selection

The Massey-Dickinson Company set up the random generator section of the ESPATESTER to automatically produce a new target every one-tenth of a second. The targets were the digits zero through four. The first nine rows of table 12 represent the cumulated sums of frequencies of occurrence of the five possible targets. The tenth row shows the frequencies of occurrence of a very much longer run of 302,311 selections, independent of the first series of 7,359 selections. Means are rounded off to the nearest unit.

The requirements for ESPATESTER call for the probability of each target selected being equal (in this case each probability being .2). A Chi-square test of the 7,359 selections series indicates that the observed values do not depart significantly from this model (Chi-square $= 4.047$ with 4 d.f., and P is approximately equal to .35, 2-tailed). A similar Chi-square test of fit of the much larger series in the tenth row of table 12 is also non-significant (Chi-square $= 6.249$ with 4 d.f., and P is approximately equal to .15, 2-tailed). While it would be more satisfactory to have the probability of this second set somewhat higher, the variation is probably only a chance deviation, for the "favored" target in the second series is not the favored target in the first series, and the least-favored targets also change identity between the series.

ESPATESTER Parts List

Massey-Dickinson Equipment

1	Counter-Stepper, cs-34
1	Lamp Driver, 6 module, id-41
1	Output Control, medium duty (2DPDT reed relays), r-42
1	Input Modifier-Delay, d-14
2	Electromechanical Counter (2 counters/module) emc-40
1	Multiple AND Gate (6 two-legged gates/module), mc-27
1	Inhibited AND Gate, ic-21
1	OR Gate, or-22
1	Power Supply, p-4
78	Patch Cords
4	Middle Rails, r-76C
1	Top Rail, r-76A
1	Bottom Power Rail, r-76B

} for mounting above equipment

Other Components

1	S1, 2, 3, 4, 5	5-button push switch, mechanically interlocked to prevent more than one switch being pressed at a time. *Switchcraft* 'Multiswitch' line suitable
5	RY.1, 2, 3, 4, 5	DPDT relay, mercury wetted contacts, 24 VDC coil, such as Potter-Brumfield JM2-1-9-22, or Clare HG2A-1003-2A2
10	R1 to 10	10,000 ohm 2 watt potentiometers, linear taper
5	L1, 2, 3, 4, 5	Pilot light bulbs, types 320, 327, 334, 335, or 1829
1	C1	.05 uf, 600VDC paper capacitor
1	R11	1,000 ohm, ½W
1	B1	3VDC battery

References

Banham, K. 1970. The effect of feedback on guessing. *J. Parapsychol.* 34:226.

———. 1973. Feedback, learning, and guessing. *J. Parapsychol.* 37:72-73.

Beloff, J. 1969. The "sweethearts" experiment. *J. Soc. Psych. Res.* 45:1-7.

Beloff, J., and Bate, D. 1971. An attempt to replicate the Schmidt findings. *J. Soc. Psych. Res.* 46:21-30.

Beloff, J., and Regan, T. 1969. The Edinburgh electronic ESP tester. *J. Soc. Psych. Res.* 45:7-13.

Brugmans, H. 1922. Une communication sur des expériences télépathiques au laboratoire de Psychologie à Groningue faites par M. Heymans, Docteur Weinberg et Docteur H. I. F. W. Brugmans. *Le Compte Rendu Officiel du Premier Congrès International des Recherches Psychiques.* Copenhagen.

Cutten, J. H. 1961. "ESPIAR" (ESP indicator and recorder). *J. Soc. Psych. Res.* 41:32-41.

Dagle, L. 1968. The effect of immediate reinforcement in a two-choice ESP test. Master's thesis, Trinity University.

Dagle, L., and Puryear, H. 1969. The effects of immediate reinforcement in a two-choice GESP test. *J. Parapsychol.* 33:339 (abstract).

Dale, L., Taves, E., and Murphy, G. 1944. Research notes. *J. Amer. Soc. Psych. Res.* 38:160-70.

Drucker, S., and Drewes, A. 1976 (forthcoming). Return of the m&m's: a further study of ESP in relation to cognitive development. In *Research in Parapsychology 1975*, ed. J. Morris, W. Roll, and R. Morris. Metuchen, N.J.: Scarecrow Press.

Fouts, G. 1973. The effect of reinforcement on telepathic behavior.

Paper read at Rocky Mountain Psychol. Assn., 1973, Las Vegas, Nevada.

Haraldsson, E. 1970. Subject selection in a machine precognition test. *J. Parapsychol.* 34:182–91.

Hilgard, E. 1962. *Introduction to psychology.* New York: Harcourt, Brace & World.

Honorton, C. 1970. Effects of feedback on discrimination between correct and incorrect ESP responses. *J. Amer. Soc. Psych. Res.* 64:404–10.

———. 1971a. Effects of feedback on discrimination between correct and incorrect ESP responses: a replication study. *J. Amer. Soc. Psych. Res.* 65:155–61.

———. 1971b. Automated forced-choice precognition tests with a "sensitive." *J. Amer. Soc. Psych. Res.* 65:476–81.

Honorton, C., Ramsey, M., and Cabibbo, C. 1975. Experimenter effects in extrasensory perception. *J. Amer. Soc. Psych. Res.* 69: 135–50.

Humphrey, B. 1948. *Handbook of tests in parapsychology.* Durham, N.C.: Parapsychology Laboratory.

Humphrey, B., and Nicol, J. 1955. The feeling of success in ESP. *J. Amer. Soc. Psych. Res.* 49:3–37.

Jampolsky, G., and Haight, M. 1975. A pilot study of ESP in hyperkinetic children. In *Research in Parapsychology 1974,* ed. J. Morris, W. Roll, and R. Morris, Metuchen, N.J.: Scarecrow Press.

Kanthamani, H., and Kelly, E. 1974. Card experiments with a special subject. I. Single-card clairvoyance. *J. Parapsychol.* 38: 16–26.

Kelly, E., and Kanthamani, B. 1972. A subject's efforts toward voluntary control. *J. Parapsychol.* 36:185–97.

Kreiman, N., and Ivnisky, D. 1973. Effects of feedback on ESP responses. *Cuadernos de Parapsicologia.* 6 (no. 2):1–10. *J. Parapsychol.* 37:367 (abstract).

Kreitler, H., and Kreitler, S. 1972. Does extrasensory perception affect psychological experiments? *J. Parapsychol.* 36:1–45.

Lewis, L., and Schmeidler, G. 1971. Alpha relations with nonintentional and purposeful ESP after feedback. *J. Amer. Soc. Psych. Res.* 65:455–67.

Lübke, C., and Rohr, W. 1975. Psi and subliminal perception: a replication of the Kreitler and Kreitler study. In *Research in Parapsychology 1974,* ed. J. Morris, W. Roll, and R. Morris, pp. 161-64. Metuchen, N.J.: Scarecrow Press.

McCallam, E., and Honorton, C. 1973. Effects of feedback on discrimination between correct and incorrect ESP responses: a further replication and extension. *J. Amer. Soc. Psych. Res.* 67: 77-85.

Mercer, S. 1967. Instrumental conditioning in a GESP experiment. *J. Parapsychol.* 31:83-84.

Mitchell, E. 1971. An ESP test from Apollo 14. *J. Parapsychol.* 35: 89-107.

Morgan, C. 1956. *Introduction to psychology.* New York: McGraw-Hill.

Murphy, G., and Taves, E. 1942. Current plans for investigation in psychical research. *J. Amer. Soc. Psych. Res.* 36:15-28.

Ojha, A. 1964. Amount of knowledge in ESP and guessing situations. *J. Gen. Psychol.* 71:307-12.

Orne, M. 1962. On the social psychology of the psychological experiment: with particular reference to demand characteristics and their implications. *Amer. Psychologist* 17:776-83.

Pratt, J. 1949. The meaning of performance curves in ESP and PK test data. *J. Parapsychol.* 13:9-22.

Price, G. 1955. Science and the supernatural. *Science* 122: 359-67.

Puharich, A. 1973. *Beyond telepathy.* New York: Doubleday.

Rand Corporation. 1955. *A million random digits.* Glencoe, Ill: Free Press.

Rhine, J. 1939. Requirements and suggestions for an ESP test machine. *J. Parapsychol.* 3:3-10.

Rosenthal, R. 1966. *Experimenter effects in behavioral research.* New York: Appleton-Century-Crofts.

Sanford, J., and Keil, H. 1975. The effect of "normal" vs. relaxed states of consciousness on ESP scoring using a GESP feedback testing device. In *Research in Parapsychology 1974,* ed. J. Morris, W. Roll, and R. Morris, pp. 24-27. Metuchen, N.J.: Scarecrow Press.

Schmeidler, G., and Lewis, L. 1968. A search for feedback in ESP: Part II. High ESP scores after two successes on triple-aspect targets. *J. Amer. Soc. Psych. Res.* 62:255-62.

Schmeidler, G., and McConnell, R. 1958. *ESP and personality patterns*. New Haven: Yale University Press.

Schmidt, H. 1969a. Precognition of a quantum process. *J. Parapsychol.* 33:99–108.

———. 1969b. Clairvoyance tests with a machine. *J. Parapsychol.* 33:300–306.

———. 1969c. Quantum processes predicted. *New Scientist* 44: 114–16.

———. 1970a. The psi quotient (PQ): an efficiency measure for psi tests. *J. Parapsychol.* 34:210–14.

———. 1970b. A quantam mechanical random number generator for psi tests. *J. Parapsychol.* 34:219–24.

———. 1973. PK tests with a high-speed random number generator. *J. Parapsychol.* 37:105–18.

Schmidt, H., and Pantas, L. 1972. Psi tests with internally different machines. *J. Parapsychol.* 36:222–32.

Siegel, S. 1956. *Non-parametric statistics for the behavorial sciences*. New York: McGraw-Hill.

Smith, W. R., and others. 1963. *Testing for extrasensory perception with a machine*. Bedford, Mass.: Air Force Cambridge Research Laboratories.

Stewart, W. C. 1959. Three new ESP test machines and some preliminary results. *J. Parapsychol.* 23:44–48.

Targ, R., and Hurt, D. 1972. Use of an automatic stimulus generator to teach extrasensory perception. *Proc. IEEE International Symposium on Information Theory.*

Targ, R., Cole, P., and Puthoff, H. 1974. *Development of techniques to enhance man/machine communication.* Stanford Research Institute Project 2613 report.

Tart, C. 1963. Physiological correlates of psi cognition. *Inter. J. Parapsychol.* 5:375–86.

———. 1966a. Card guessing tests: learning paradigm or extinction paradigm? *J. Amer. Soc. Psych. Res.* 60:46–55.

———. 1966b. ESPATESTER: an automatic testing device for parapsychological research. *J. Amer. Soc. Psych. Res.* 60:256–69.

———.1966c. Models for the explanation of extrasensory perception. *Inter. J. Neuropsychiat.* 2:488–504.

———. 1973a. Parapsychology. *Science* 182:222.

———. 1973b. Preliminary notes on the nature of psi processes. In *The nature of human consciousness*, ed. R. Ornstein, pp. 468–92. San Francisco: W. H. Freeman.

————. 1975. *The application of learning theory to extrasensory perception*. New York: Parapsychology Foundation.

Taves, E. 1939. A machine for research in extrasensory perception. *J. Parapsychol.* 3:11–16.

Taves, E., and Dale, L. 1943. The Midas touch in psychical research. *J. Amer. Soc. Psych. Res.* 37:57–83.

Taves, E., Dale, L., and Murphy, G. 1943. A further report on the Midas touch. *J. Amer. Soc. Psych. Res.* 37:111–18.

Thouless, R. 1971. Experiments on psi self-training with Dr. Schmidt's precognitive apparatus. *J. Soc. Psych. Res.* 46:15–21.

Timm, U. 1973. The measurement of psi. *J. Amer. Soc. Psych. Res.* 67:282–94.

Troffer, S., and Tart, C. 1964. Experimenter bias in hypnotist performance. *Science* 145:1330–31.

Tyrrell, G. 1936–1937. Further research in extrasensory perception. *Proc. Soc. Psych. Res.* 44:99–168.

————. 1938. The Tyrrell apparatus for testing extrasensory perception. *J. Parapsychol.* 2:107–18.

Vasiliev, L. 1963. *Experiments in mental suggestion*. Church Crookham, England: Institute for the Study of Mental Images.

Walter, W. 1965. Mechanical techniques in future telepathy research. *Inter. J. Parapsychol.* 7:135–49.

Webster, D. 1949. An automatic testing and recording device for experiments in extrasensory perception. *J. Parapsychol.* 13:107–17.

White, R. 1964. A comparison of old and new methods of response to targets in ESP experiments. *J. Amer. Soc. Psych. Res.* 58:21–56.

Notes

Chapter 1.   Card Guessing Tests

1. The term *card guessing tests* is used broadly in this context to include all tests in which the subject chooses among several alternative responses on each trial.

2. We can ignore for the purposes of this discussion the use of intermittent reinforcement in psychology, for this is used only *after* some degree of learning has been brought about by constant reinforcement of correct responses.

3. Tyrrell's (1937; 1938) device seems a noteworthy exception. Here the subject tried to guess which box among several had a light on inside it. On opening the box, the subject saw immediately whether she was right or wrong. Tyrrell's tests were some of the most successful in the field, despite the drawbacks due to lack of randomicity in a number of his experiments.

4. ESPATESTER was later constructed, although I did not have time to systematically use it.

Chapter 2.   Learning Theory Application by Others

1. The literature on testing for psychokinesis (PK) with dice might be of help here: since subjects usually saw the dice fall, they received relatively immediate feedback. Since decline effects are almost universal in PK studies (Pratt, 1949) and the amount of PK shown is usually very small (albeit statistically significant), subjects in PK studies have generally been below the necessary "talent threshold" needed for learning. Helmut Schmidt's work is particularly relevant here, as his electronic PK machines usually provide immediate feedback, but I have not had the opportunity to adequately review the PK literature.

2. Note, however, that such testing should not be long enough to extinguish the subject's ESP talents! This is a difficult practical problem.

3. A fifth subject had to quit the experiment much sooner than the rest, so his results will be disregarded.

4. The stacking effect refers to the fact that a subject might score well on a particular run through a target series by chance, the (random) target order just happening to correspond to the subject's guessing habits on that occasion. If many subjects are guessing at that same target deck and they happen to have similar guessing habits (which is possible for people from the same culture), this chance success might stack up across subjects and thus erroneously inflate results.

5. Schmeidler and Lewis (1968) also carried out a study where the feedback seemed variably delayed rather than immediate, so it is not reviewed here.

6. Since the exponential notation I use in this book for very small probability figures might not be familiar to all readers, a word of explanation is in order. A probability figure expressed in the form $N \times 10^{-X}$ means that the probability of the observed result occurring by chance is the number N, with the decimal point and number of zeros between N and the decimal point expressed by x. So 4×10^{-2} could be written out as .04, 8×10^{-6} as .000008, and so forth. The exponential method is convenient in avoiding the writing and counting of long strings of zeros.

7. This incident is a nice illustration of the psychology of belief. Psychologists routinely believe cheating goes on in parapsychological studies if there are not rigid safeguards. The second subject is a personal friend of mine and a highly respected psychologist; he doesn't think *his* self-recorded results should be discounted in this way!

8. The machine used by Targ and Hurt was a prototype of the Aquarius Model 100 ESP Trainer, described later. My son David discovered it was possible to cheat on this machine in the precognition mode to get one extra hit per trial. I have contacted the manufacturer to have this defect remedied. Whether this might have been possible on Targ's and Hurt's prototype machine is doubtful, for their data indicate a fairly steady upswing in performance rather than a sudden step and then steadiness.

Chapter 3.   A Pilot Study: Psi-Missing and Fear of Psi

1. When total ESP trials are not fixed beforehand, the question arises as to whether positive results are due to selective stopping, i.e., subjects quitting right after a run of "chance luck." This does not seem to be the case here. The most successful subject stopped because of emotional upset, and five of the other nine subjects were showing mildly upward or steady trends when they stopped. Stopping was primarily a matter of the experimenters and subjects not having time to do further work.

Chapter 4.   A Three-Stage Study in Training ESP Ability

1. One subgroup used the 25 Zener card deck in its testing; statistically this procedure is identical with the main one, only the particular symbols used being different.

2. About one-third of the way through the training phase, the Aquarius machine broke down and began repeating one target with a very high frequency. The experimenters immediately spotted this and the data from these runs were discarded. The machine was repaired at the factory and showed satisfactory randomicity before being used again.

3. Randomicity was tested for both training machines by recording 1,000 consecutive targets. These data were tested with a Chi-square test for equal frequency of single targets, to be certain no particular targets were favored or underpresented, and with a Chi-square test for equal frequency of all possible pair sequences of targets, to be sure of serial independence.

We also decided, before beginning the study, that the randomicity tests were to be carried out on the equipment before and after the experiment, but not with data obtained when subjects were actually trying to use ESP. Since we do not understand how ESP works, and since the literature shows that subjects often use extrasensory and psychokinetic abilities in ways other than what they are consciously intending to do, we thought it might be possible for subjects to unknowingly affect the random generators psychokinetically during the actual experiment. We have since learned that Schmidt and Pantas (1972) have demonstrated precisely this by obtaining significant results in a study where subjects believed they were *guessing* the state of the electronic random number generator but actually they had to psychokinetically affect it in order to score above chance. A detailed analysis for such effects in the present study will be presented in a future publication by Lila Gatlin.

4. After the completion of the Training Study, I realized that this procedure allowed a possibility of sensory cueing. If a particular experimenter showed a differential time delay between reading the output of the random number generator and switching on various newly selected targets, a subject might become sensitive to this and artifactually increase his score. This is quite unlikely, as there was a variable delay between writing down target and response, switching off the previous target, and pushing the selection button on the random number generator which would obscure any consistent differences in the time delay between reading the output of the random number generator and switching on the newly selected target. Indeed, El (Gaines Thomas) reports in chapter 5 that he took variable lengths of time to switch on targets, as he needed varying lengths of time to "fix" the target in his mind before switching on the TCT. Nevertheless, we hypothesized that there might be a longer delay in switching on targets whose switches were furthest from the random number generator (thus requiring a longer hand motion by the experimenter) that would make these targets more discriminable to subjects or, more generally, that El might have inadvertently used some consistent code of this sort which would have cued his subjects and thus inflated scores. We examined the results of the five subjects of El who scored significantly on the TCT in the Training Study, but found no consistent differential pattern at all across these subjects as to which targets they scored best or worst on, so this theoretically possible hypothesis received no empirical support. Nevertheless, this possibility should be eliminated in future work, and in appendix 1 a simple modification of the TCT is described which makes the time delay between switching off one target and selecting the next uniform and beyond the experimenter-sender's control.

5. The "feel" some subjects searched for was not a perception of the DC electrostatic field from the selected (but unlit) target lamp. The circuit of the TCT (see appendix 1) had the base filament connection of all target lamps connected to a common line, with a lamp being lit after a response by connecting the common line to the -24VDC lead of the power supply, so the electrostatic field at each of the ten unlit target lamps would be identical. Target lamps were partially recessed in a metal panel and covered with a plastic diffusing dome. Probing with a finger-size electrode, connected to a VTVM, shunted with body-equivalent resistance to ground, and capable of detecting 10 millivolt potentials, showed no measurable potentials on either the TCT or Aquarius machines.

6. The manufacturer can now modify the Aquarius trainer so the experimenter-sender must push a button to select the next target.

7. As mentioned before, procedurally these were telepathy runs, although we cannot rule out direct clairvoyant perception of the state of the machine. With the Aquarius, subjects may often have been using clairvoyance simply because by working very fast they did not give the experimenter-senders any real chance to focus on sending.

8. After the study was completed, we discovered that one subject, S12, had done only 19 runs, through experimenter oversight, but we decided to include his results anyway. This decision was made before any analysis had been carried out. As it turned out, exclusion of his results would not have materially affected our findings.

9. The experimenters who ran subjects completely through the Training Study were Alan Croft, Bruce Frankel, Mark Glatt, David Kraus, Eric Larsen, Judi Norquist, Frank Odasz, Dana Redington, Gaines Thomas, Ryan Unruh, and Mark Watts. Irene Segrest assisted in all aspects of the study.

10. In the original monograph reporting these results (Tart, 1975), one-tailed tests were mistakenly used. This made for trivial differences in most cases, but it does account for some variations between this report and the original work.

11. In inspecting the data sheets of the 11 TCT subjects who did not complete the Training Study, 7 of them had only one run each. A retrospective checking (after main data analysis had been completed) showed that these were children from a local school who were being screened on the TCT without any previous testing or selection, so their data do not really belong in the Training Study analyses. We let the figures stand as is in table 5 simply to account for all data. If the data of these 7 subjects were removed, the TCT results for the remaining subjects would be 811 hits in 230 runs, $P = 2 \times 10^{-24}$, so leaving them in or taking them out makes no practical difference.

12. The significance of slopes was tested using a standard table for the associated correlation coefficients.

13. A sign test on the slopes would not take into account the large magnitude differences among them.

14. If the data of three subjects who failed to complete the Training Study but had enough runs (8, 14, and 14) to allow a reasonable estimate of overall slope are added in, this correlation becomes +.26.

15. Two incomplete subjects had enough runs (10, 10) to allow a reasonable slope estimate. If these data are added in, the correlation is +.64, a negligible change.

16. N is 10 rather than 8 here, for two subjects did only one run each on the TCT in the Confirmation Study; while this was used as a best score, it was not used as a mean.

17. These means are slightly different from those in the previous paragraph because here the analysis uses only subjects who worked on both devices, while in the previous analysis a few subjects are included who worked on only one or the other device.

Chapter 6.   Discussions and Conclusions

1. I have not included the much older studies reviewed in chapter 1, as I put less reliance on very old data. Their inclusion would not have changed any conclusions, however.

2. Although the Ojha (1964), Fouts (1973), and Dagle (1968) studies are included in table 10 for reference, I have not included their data in this or subsequent calculations due to their methodological flaws.

Appendix 1.   The Ten-Choice Trainer

1. Since the pilot light fixtures used protruded about half an inch above the panel face, the reader might wonder if subjects who tried to "feel" for the correct target might have actually been detecting an electrostatic field from the selected (albeit

unlit) target lamp through some little-known cutaneous sense, rather than using ESP with the idea of a "feeling" being only a convenient readout mechanism for the subject's ESP abilities. The TCT was designed to avoid this possibility. Referring back to figure 21, note that the bases of all 10 target lamps were connected to a common line, and that this common line was not connected to the -24VDC power bus until a response button was pressed. Thus, even though power from the +24VDC bus was applied to the filament of the selected target, this same voltage was, in terms of possible electrostatic fields, applied to *all* target lamp filaments equally. Thus the TCT presented a flat metal face with all circuitry shielded except an equal, minute electrostatic field theoretically occurring at each of the target lamps where the lamp filament (inside its glass bulb in turn inside a plastic shield, the pilot lamp fixture diffusing shield) protruded about an eighth of an inch through the panel.

Appendix 2.   ESPATESTER

1. My particular thanks go to Herbert Bello and Robert Bello of the Massey-Dickinson Company (9 Elm Street, Saxonville, Massachusetts) for their aid in designing the ESPATESTER with standard Massey-Dickinson components.

2. By instructing the subject to depress his button longer for those guesses about which he is more confident, an automatic scoring of confidence can be accomplished.

3. At 1966 prices.

4. Five target possibilities are used because this number is common to most ESP studies. The device can select from 2 to 10 targets. With the purchase of additional equipment, it could select from hundreds.

5. These relays are used to eliminate "contact bounce" in the switches. Five additional Input Modifier-Delay units could be used instead. This would eliminate much of the soldering required in constructing ESPATESTER, but at considerable expense.

6. Helmut Schmidt has now designed and tested a number of randomizing and ESP testing devices using the rate of radioactive decay as the randomizing source, and the investigator planning to construct testing and training machines in this area should consult his work (Schmidt, 1970b; 1973; Schmidt & Pantas, 1972).

7. It would also be possible to write out the target selection and responses on a 10-channel even marker polygraph, and some investigators might prefer this.

8. This is redundant, but convenient information.

9. The presence of capacitor C1 across the target indicating output eliminates the "hash" that would otherwise appear during the selection process, thus assuring a clean polygraph record.

Index